RESPONSIBILITY
REBORN

"John Andrews has made a valuable contribution that all Americans should read. His work bears out Ronald Reagan's conviction that the best is yet to come for America. We need a rebirth of personal responsibility, and this timely book shows the way."

—Edwin Meese III, Attorney General under President Reagan

"John Andrews shines a light on our failings as well as providing a beacon of hope for America's future. You will be inspired."

—Hank Brown, Former President, University of Colorado, and former U.S. Senator

"Memo to those under 40: personal responsibility was something expected of Americans—before we all became 'dysfunctional' and 'victims,' blaming others for the consequences of wrong choices. In this book, John Andrews reminds us what our grandparents regarded as self-evident truth, and plots a way towards a future when taking responsibility will improve both our individual lives and national life."

—Cal Thomas, Syndicated Columnist and Fox News Contributor

"Self-doubt is epidemic in our land, and critics of America abound. In this gracefully written and keenly analyzed chronicle of our times, John Andrews counters with a positive vision for the future—concluding with ten steps each of us can take to help realize a better America."

—Donald Hodel, Secretary of the Interior under President Reagan

"In his 'love letter to my country,' Andrews draws upon his life of extensive study and practical experience to issue a call to personal responsibility for every citizen. 'Our toughest challenges now are not political,' he reasons, 'They are moral.' Right on! Andrews correctly identifies individual citizen responsibility as the key to American exceptionalism in centuries past and the century ahead."

—Bob Beauprez, Former Congressman

"From a veteran of the front lines in the battle for America comes a fresh appraisal of the challenges we face and what we must do to win. My friend John Andrews draws upon his rich experiences as a White House speechwriter, state legislator, think tank executive, committed family man, and lifelong activist to offer up a compelling message: Freedom is not automatic. It cannot survive in a dangerous world if people shirk their responsibility or compromise their character. Rolling back the forces that are ravaging the American Dream—from big government to family breakdown to the disintegration of education—requires a sober analysis and a solid battle plan. With this book, freedom-loving Americans can win back their country and their future."

—Lawrence W. Reed, President, Foundation for Economic Education

"No stranger to the rough and tumble of national and state politics, John Andrews offers a non-partisan clarion call for the recovery of citizenship. 'The Spirit of '76' was staked on what the American Founders called 'public virtue' or the values necessary for citizenship. They believed that responsibility is integral to political rights. So does Andrews. *Responsibility Reborn* offers a pathway for renewing the civic vision of the Founders in America's third century. I recommend it highly to anyone of goodwill seeking to effectively engage the crises of our hour."

—Alan R. Crippen II, President, John Jay Institute for Faith, Society, and Law

"Americans contemplate the state of the Republic today and wonder why we have strayed so far from the Founders' vision of a federation of self-governing individuals, families, and communities to our current condition of widespread dependency and disillusionment. John Andrews draws on a lifetime of striving and accomplishment to focus on one often-neglected element in the mix—that of personal responsibility. Andrews underscores his points with a frank self-assessment of his own strivings to practice responsibility guided by his faith, sometimes with success and sometimes falling short. Not for him the weaselly equivocations of so many political autobiographies. *Responsibility Reborn* is an unusually honest meditation on this ancient virtue."

—James C. Bennett, Author, *The Anglosphere Challenge: Why the English-Speaking Nations Will Lead the Way in the 21st Century*

"*Responsibility Reborn* is a clear and convincing explanation of what ails our country and how to fix it. John Andrews is a celebrated public intellectual, a patriot, and an excellent writer. His new book is a huge encouragement to those of us who love our country."

—Bill Armstrong, President, Colorado Christian University, and former U.S. Senator

"John Andrews' *Responsibility Reborn* is good reading, with interesting insights into a history he and I share. It's a clarion call for all Americans to transcend ideology and self-absorption by re-embracing personal responsibility toward our neighbors and our nation. Without personal responsibility, self-government doesn't work. It's that simple, and John's excellent book nails it."

—Chuck Colson, Founder, Prison Fellowship, and former Special Counsel to President Richard Nixon

"John Andrews is a remarkable man and an unselfish servant of the good. His book reminds us that a significant life requires responsibility to duty more than anything else. Young, ambitious people ought to be combing through *Responsibility Reborn*—and not just conservatives, but everyone who aims to lead and to leave behind a worthy legacy from having led."

—Hugh Hewitt, Author and Syndicated Radio Host

RESPONSIBILITY
REBORN

A Citizen's Guide
to the Next American Century

JOHN ANDREWS

Foreword by Hugh Hewitt

DENALI
PRESS

A Division of MT6 Media, Inc.

DENALI
PRESS

A Division of MT6 Media, Inc.

5445 DTC Parkway
Penthouse Four
Greenwood Village, Colorado 80111
www.MT6Media.com

ISBN: 978-0-9836390-0-8

Printed in the United States

To my parents, John and Marianne Andrews,
and my wife's parents, Morton and Patricia D'Evelyn:
quiet heroes of responsibility all

CONTENTS

UP THE HILL

In the course of 11 years on the radio and ten before that on television, I have met and interviewed—and this is a conservative count—ten thousand individuals. That number doesn't include callers.

That's the backdrop for my opening statement about John Andrews: He has led a remarkable life, one that includes plunging to the depths of the seas and serving in the highest halls of power at 1600 Pennsylvania Avenue, a career that combined a hike up "Mount Governor," as John calls it, in which he "failed to summit," and an extraordinary run as the conscience of Colorado conservatives and leader of a great legislative body.

John Andrews is a remarkable man, and a good friend, but mostly he is an unselfish servant of the good—not a perfect servant, as he is quick to point out in *Responsibility Reborn*—but a dedicated and tireless servant.

I have known John for a decade, but when I put down this book I knew not just John and his wife Donna much better, but also Colorado and indeed the post-war United States. There is valuable, hard-won insight in every chapter, along with pointers to fascinating people and to important books like Sir John Glubb's *The Fate of Empires*. But the book's most lasting contribution for me will be its steady reminder that a significant life requires responsibility to duty more than anything else.

John Andrews and I both served Richard Nixon as writers—John while RN was in the White House, and I during his exile years in San Clemente after the fall. So there is much in the book for anyone who wants to understand what happened to America during Vietnam and Watergate. The most interesting insights, though, are about what happens to people, for good and bad, when they live at or near the summit of power in federal or state governments.

Young, ambitious people ought to be combing through *Responsibility Reborn*—and not just conservatives, but everyone who aims to lead and to leave behind a worthy legacy from having led.

John Andrews conducts an "ethical autopsy" on his life up until now, and given his new adventures and vigorous schedule, we can assume that this is only Part 1—a mid-term test of sorts. What comes of the effort is a model of candor and good humor, seriousness and substance, that will prod every reader to undertake a similar evaluation. "If I could write as well as John Andrews," the reader will be thinking, "how would my report card turn out?"

John aims to provoke here, to prod his readers and especially his Colorado readers, to begin to study their own responsibility for the variety of ditches into which the state and nation have driven in recent years, and the failure to summit in so many areas. There isn't an ounce of vindictiveness in this memoir *cum* exhortation, just a patient, smiling, and gentle (most of the time) hand-on-the-back push up the hill.

HUGH HEWITT
Newport Beach, California
April 2011

DESTINATION 2076

"We need a new force in American politics," wrote an ex-legislator turned newspaper columnist in July 2007. Polls showed voters unhappy with presidential contenders from both parties.

But the pundit and former state Senate president (this writer) said there was no need for a new party. Instead, the column argued, "We need a responsibility movement to challenge both parties and reach beyond them. We'll call it Element R and launch it today, right here in Colorado."

That was one of the best-received articles I've published in six years as a Denver Post contributor, probably because I played against type and looked at things from outside the customary right-left ideological framework. Our bipartisan responsibility deficit has become my theme in a series of columns since then.

Did the idea of Element R cause a political earthquake? No, and it probably never will. But so many kindred spirits respond, every time it's mentioned, that I wanted to put together this handbook for our mutual encouragement.

Does my vision for a new responsibility movement signal a change of beliefs for someone who has been a soldier in the conservative movement since the days of Barry Goldwater, and a lifelong disciple of America's founding principles? Absolutely not. The old self-evident truths remain, of that I am sure.

But I am concerned that if we don't find a more positive, less polarizing way to express and apply those truths, Americans will lose hold of them. "Responsibility reborn" is a fresh way of thinking about our country, our history, our form of government, and the lives we lead together. "Responsibility reborn" also illuminates my life story, I have realized. Might it do the same for yours?

THE PATH OF THE BOOK

Thank you for picking up this book by an unknown author and venturing to think with me about the implications of Element R—past, present, and future. If I could sketch the path we will take in a couple of hundred words, it is this:

I will argue that personal responsibility, the determination to do the right thing by choice, is the quintessential American character trait. It has been the mainspring of our nation's greatness from earliest times. Its rebirth has pulled us out of decline since the disastrous 1960s and '70s.

Freedom and responsibility are inseparable. America's founders knew this—knew it with a certainty I have come to share through a lifetime in conservative politics. True personal responsibility is the only way forward for the United States in the 21st century.

As citizens, we must rededicate ourselves to a responsibility ethic. And we must reject counterfeit collective responsibility—mass obligation imposed by government. The three sections that follow are intended to help us do that.

The section on "Convictions" establishes responsibility and irresponsibility as main themes for understanding what we, our parents, and our grandparents have lived through in the past American century. Those themes are first analyzed through the lens of history and political thought. Then they are illustrated by some highs and lows from my own political career.

The next section, "Lessons," takes a rapid scan of the author's career, in order to set up a responsibility self-appraisal for one

American looking back—followed by some thoughts on what personal responsibility must mean for all of us, looking ahead.

The final section on "Responsibilities" caps off our citizen's guide with an account of how this country overcame its near-fatal responsibility deficit in the late 20th century. I conclude with a 10-point responsibility agenda for Americans in this new century, as a decisive decade now unfolds.

UNCLE SAM IS BACK

When I was a boy in the years after World War II, Henry Luce and *Time* magazine proclaimed the 20th century as the American century. But that boast sounded hollow by the time this kid from Backbone, Colorado, was serving as a presidential speechwriter on the eve of our 1976 bicentennial. Irresponsibility reached its worst amid the agony of Vietnam and Watergate. The United States was being written off.

Thankfully—and, some would say, surprisingly—our country has experienced a rebirth of responsibility since then. Uncle Sam is back. It's now realistic to think of the new chapter stretching toward 2076 as the *next* American century. It has been citizens like you, people who loved their heritage and knew their duty, who brought us this far. Here is my rough draft on a guide for the road ahead.

You and I probably won't see the tricentennial of the Declaration of Independence, even with today's increasing life spans. Our children and their children will be here for the birthday, though. If the United States reaches that notable anniversary, as we pray she does, it will be because countless citizens kept working toward an ideal called responsible America.

Not Republican or Democratic America, conservative or liberal America, religious or secular America, but *responsible* America. A place where rights are secure, and things tend to turn out right, because individuals and institutions work to *do right*.

Doing right: that doesn't seem a lot to ask. Yet amazingly, no other country defines itself by that standard as ours does. On these shores there is a personal and communal expectation of character and moral integrity like nowhere else. It is our great national treasure.

But even here, responsibility always fights an undertow—temptation, weariness, aging. Responsibility is in need of rebirth again and again. That's human nature. Thus "responsibility reborn" is not only a theme verse for my own and our country's experience over the past generation. It is also a charge to keep for generations of Americans to come.

At mid-century, decades from now, my son's son Ian Andrews may be in law enforcement like his dad or in health care like his mother. He may be in business or politics, education or ministry, as his grandfathers were. But whatever path in life Ian takes, he and his contemporaries will still have a citizens' test to meet. They will still have to measure up to the responsibility ethic day by day.

It has never been easy and never will be. No one gets a pass. This will *only* be the next American century if you and I along with our neighbors and our descendants, the infant born today and the immigrant arriving tomorrow, all do our part to make it that.

Fortunately, much has already been done to exemplify and advance responsible America for us. We have great role models of responsibility in the near and distant past, as well as some living now. We stand on the shoulders of giants. What an honor and a blessing to be citizens of the United States of America in this new millennium.

ALMOST CHOSEN

Are we Americans a chosen people? No. Can those among us who follow a biblical faith, as I do, claim special anointing for the civil government we have inherited? No.

But we might indeed be, as the unchurched Lincoln put it, an "almost-chosen people."[1] Many of us, from varying religious traditions, sense a unique opportunity and obligation for Americans to serve the Almighty's benevolent purposes in a broken world.

I personally think Lincoln was right—though these pages are not about my Christian beliefs. They are simply about a beautiful thing called responsibility, a beautiful time called now, and a beautiful place called America.

"America the Beautiful" was written atop Pike's Peak, as we Coloradans like to remind the other states. A schoolteacher named Katharine Lee Bates penned the lines in 1893. Anybody who has been to a mountaintop can identify with the mixture of moods Bates evokes, a mixture echoed in this book—aspiration and inspiration, celebration and meditation, panorama and petition.

Lincoln had it right

The high peaks are not really her poem's subject, however. We the people are. Reading the lyrics, you realize that Bates' tribute is to the soul-beauty of Americans, the gold of our nobleness.[2] She hymns the pilgrims and heroes of our past, the gleaming cities of our future.

She prays for us as citizens, that by divine grace our flaws would be mended, our selfishness subdued, our self-control strengthened. Her eight verses could really be summed up in a couple of words: Responsibility reborn.

Our good land under the spacious skies is no Oz. The real America we live in is not all fruitfulness and alabaster. Yesterdays without regrets don't figure in our patriot dream. Nor do tomorrows without tears. But *doing right* does figure in that dream.

Are Americans capable of the "nobler" citizenship that Katharine Bates proclaimed in her time, and for which I have envisioned a responsibility movement in our time? I am convinced we are. And if we want the USA to see 2076, nothing less will suffice.

I write this as citizen to citizen with gratitude for the brotherhood that crowns us; with awe at the rebirth we've seen; with urgency for the decades to come, and with conviction for the duty we bear. On that note—conviction—the book begins.

PART ONE

CONVICTIONS

CHAPTER 1

WE ARE STEWARDS

I Corinthians 4:2 [3]

Why does so much of the world want to be like America? Why do people from everywhere flock to come here? Because America is the land of opportunity. Here individuals have the best chance to become what they long to be.

Opportunity means two things: the freedom to rise and the responsibility to try. You can go as far as vision and hard work will take you. But here's something odd: While everyone talks about freedom, responsibility is seldom discussed these days.

Responsible America, the place where stepping up and doing the right thing used to be second nature, may sound like a bygone relic of the past—simplistic and square, outmoded and unrealistic. Yet even as you are reading this, an immigrant somewhere is *risking his life* in hope of making a new start on U.S. soil. Our unique American blend of freedom and responsibility remains so attractive that policymakers struggle with the problem of keeping people *out*.

Despite being written off not so long ago, it turns out that responsible America is still the hope of mankind, as well as the pride of its citizens. In the following pages, this proud citizen offers a love letter to my country.

I love the way she brings out the best in people—their nobler side, their responsible side. I am speechless with gratitude at the opportunities she's given *me*, including many second chances. I marvel at her adaptive institutions and her resilient ideals, reasserting world leadership in this new century and repeatedly disproving predictions of decline.

My impulse, like that of any lover, is to hire a plane and sky-write my praises of the beloved for everyone to see, so dazzled am I with the miracle that is America. I want my love letter about the dear land and its lifelong blessings to one citizen to be timeless enough for my little grandson Ian to read to his grandson some day.

So I write with a view to the far horizon, looking back and looking ahead, like a Colorado vista from one of our backbone summits. Yet like any book on public affairs, this one is also conditioned by circumstances. It dates from the opening phase of an historic presidency— what some observers have called the Age of Obama. To a lot of us, that dawning age felt like darkness.

PARTY'S OVER

The Republican election night party was like a wake. Everywhere you looked in the crowded, flag-draped hall on the evening of November 4, 2008, TV screens were putting up vote numbers as ugly as the stock indexes had been a month earlier. Log onto any of the big political websites for some hope of a trend in the other direction, and all you got was more of the same. Long faces predominated. What few smiles I saw were beer-induced. Laughter rose only to gallows humor.

Not since 1964 had Colorado given a presidential majority to the Democrats.[4] But on this night it was all Barack Obama. Riding his coattails from Denver to Washington, DC, were a new Democratic senator and a new Democratic congresswoman, each taking a once-safe Republican seat and symbolizing, in so doing, the expanded House and Senate majorities that would await President-elect Obama in 2009. Dems also maintained their comfortable state legislative majorities in the sweep. Liberals and conservatives fought to a draw on a dozen contentious ballot issues.

By the time GOP mourners had maxed out on masochism and the room began to empty—at no late hour—the double meaning of "party's over" had never felt truer or sadder. Heading home under a Rocky Mountain moon, I was in even lower spirits than on the night of my own defeat for governor in 1990. Then it had just been one political rookie taking his anticipated drubbing. This time it was a rout for Republicans nationally, and our side sensed a bleak finality, the end of something—not forever, of course, but maybe for a long time.

I thought back to an afternoon five years before. Two old Reagan hands, former education secretary William J. Bennett and former housing secretary Jack Kemp, were hosting a national policy conference in Aspen, August 2003. Bill Owens, Colorado's Republican governor, couldn't attend, so he delegated Senate President John Andrews and Majority Leader Mark Hillman to bring greetings to the opening reception. After adjourning the session, Bennett nodded toward Hillman and me and said to Kemp, "Keep an eye on these two guys. They're on the way to making Colorado the most conservative state in the union." We glowed with pride.

It turned out to be the pride that goes before a fall. Within weeks, two of our biggest legislative successes, the school voucher bill and the congressional redistricting bill, had fallen before the Democrat-dominated state Supreme Court. Budget woes overtook Colorado in early 2004, stalemating the legislature. Republicans lost big in that year's elections. My hope of handing the Senate gavel to one of our own as I retired on term limits was not to be. The other party took over both chambers, turning Gov. Owens' final two years into a slow defensive retreat. So much for Bill Bennett's bright prognostication. "On the way to *obscurity*" would have been more like it.

WHAT AMERICA MEANS

And yet in the big picture, so what? Political pendulums swing. Everyone knows it. That's what pendulums do. Time itself moves in only one direction, though. Actions and decisions have consequences.

Ideas have the greatest consequences of all. Some choices are fatal and there's no going back. Those are the momentous things America needs to discuss.

Another book about the back-and-forth of party combat in state capitals or in Washington, D.C., would not be worth the reader's time—and that's not this book. Although an eventful life in politics has left me with some tales to tell, they are merely incidental to my goal. My goal is for us to think together about *what America means*.

There's a bittersweet quality about the high and low moments. We can savor this by sharing it. What makes all those moments possible, though? What is the fixed point, the pivot the pendulum swings on? We had better really understand that, or we risk losing the whole thing by inattention and over-comfort.

I'll give my answer to that question right here, in case you don't read further. I actually put it in the book's title, for those who may not read this far. Personal responsibility, doing what we should—that's my answer.

- What am I responsible for? Whom am I responsible to?

- What is my reward for being responsible? What's the cost when I am irresponsible?

- Am I part of the responsibility deficit? What should I do differently? How can I know?

It's extraordinary how little thought we give these questions, when sustaining a free society is impossible unless most people get them right most of the time.

It makes far less difference which party or sect is on top, than whether individuals are practicing a responsibility ethic from the bottom up. This is the light bulb that went on for me, somewhere between the triumphal day in Aspen in 2003 and the debacle of election night 2008.

Conservatives focus a lot on liberty. Liberals focus more on equality. Yet neither is an end in itself. Liberty for what? Equality for what? The end in either case must be so that *we can live well.*

Take another contrast. Religious believers focus on merciful forgiveness. Nonbelievers, on the other hand, emphasize therapeutic nonjudgment. But here again the same question about ends and means must be asked, and the same answer—to live well—is inescapable.

The selfish and irresponsible life, the life without reciprocity or community, mocks that ideal. No matter whether we measure on a political scale from right to left, or on a spiritual scale from theism to humanism, the stern challenge to live well confronts us.

Human existence absent responsibility will inevitably become less and less human. Here is an axiom liberals and conservatives, humanists and theists alike can agree on. Here is an axis for the civilizational pendulum itself.

OBAMA ASCENDANT

Edward Hutchinson of Fennville, Michigan, my mother's brother, was a country lawyer, a state senator, and later a U.S. congressman. I marvel that it was more than half a century ago when Uncle Ed took this history-dazzled nephew from Missouri into the Michigan Senate chamber in 1958 to meet then-Gov. Mennen Williams. The memory was still vivid on a recent day when I took some students into the Colorado Senate chamber to see where President Andrews once held the gavel.

Michigan State Sen. Edward Hutchinson

It seems to me that the keynote of these fifty-plus years—the theme of my life and of our nation's life across this timespan—has been the unceasing struggle between responsibility and irresponsibility. For a time it seemed America had jettisoned the responsibility ethic. Then its advocates began to rally, with beneficial effects which I'll argue we are still experiencing.

I would like to be able to say that along this bumpy road, I always fully met my own responsibilities—but I did not. Lessons learned the hard way, for me as well as for our country, mingle ink with blood and tears in the pages that follow.

Campus radical, submariner, husband and father, presidential speechwriter, think-tank entrepreneur, writer and teacher, politician, producer and pundit, convert and missionary, seeker and adventurer, now a grandfather, mentor, and idea-broker eager for the next challenge—I have been a fortunate man.

The America I was born in, a month before D-Day, often seems light-years distant from the Facebook nation of today. Our constitution still holds, however; not only as a parchment charter but also as a compact in the hearts of the people. We are "constituted" of mutual responsibility, we Americans, and durably so.

The senescence of civilizations, diagnosed as terminal in our case not long ago, didn't take us after all. Hope remains strong here in the land of the free. Indeed "hope" now claims occupancy of the White House, albeit a hopeless pall hung over *my* party's election party in 2008.

Let's face it. Conservatives' despondency that night was not responsible, strictly speaking. We knew better. In one lifetime, mine, America has gone from a society where a Kenyan immigrant's son was unable to vote in many states or to serve in the military alongside a Michigan businessman's son, to a society where that same man could win enough of his fellow-citizens' votes to be commander-in-chief. Isn't there hope in that? I think so.

Yes, my vote was with John McCain. But anyone can see that the 2008 election reflects extremely well on our country in many ways. The racial healing evidenced in Barack Obama's remarkable run to victory, a scant 40 years after Dr. King died and the cities burned, is extraordinary by global and historical standards. It's one more example of how a freshly-energized responsibility ethic may still take the nation higher toward our finest ideals, regardless of partisan infighting along the way.

"The Age of Obama" is inevitably a catch-phrase now. Arguably, though, history may marvel more at the Age of Responsibility Reborn, our country's improbable comeback from the lows of the latter 20th century and upward into the possibilities of this new millennium. The responsibility movement for American renewal is bigger than any person, party, or presidency.

Element R, a returning seriousness in the American mind if not an actual movement in the streets, invites all of us and needs all of us. It has done much already, but much remains to be done. If it fails, we will have failed our forebears and our descendants. We will have failed a watching world. If it prevails, who knows what good may come to mankind through our responsible stewardship of that heritage our Founders called "the blessings of liberty."

For stewards we are. No smugness accompanies my belief that you and I are living in the next American century. With that privilege come solemn obligations. Citizenship involves a pledge of allegiance. A proper love letter includes the plighting of a troth, fidelity sealed. "Send me," says the ancient avowal of readiness.[5] Whither are we now sent—and for what?

CHAPTER 2

IRRESPONSIBILITY
CORRODES CITIZENSHIP

Proverbs 6:10, 11

olitical scientist Thomas Krannawitter, my colleague at Colorado
Christian University, distills the essentials of American citizenship down to four indispensable attributes. Each citizen, argues Krannawitter, must exercise *self-assertion* to defend our liberties against
intrusive government; *self-restraint* to control our baser impulses;
self-reliance to survive and thrive in freedom; and *civic knowledge* to
participate wisely in democracy.[6]

Responsible America, as I use the term, means the whole society
and body politic of individual citizens conducting themselves responsibly in each of these ways. The standard described by Krannawitter
is simple but demanding. The closer we approach it individually, the
more our government and civic institutions will be found conducting themselves responsibly toward "we the people" and among the
community of nations. Countless small acts of responsibility or irresponsibility are aggregated into a more responsible or less responsible
United States, domestically and internationally.

The low point of American irresponsibility in the past hundred
years was the decade of the 1970s. The low point of that decade, as far
as citizenship and constitutional government were concerned, was the
sordid episode in which the 37th President, heir of Washington and

31

Lincoln, was reduced to insisting on national television, "I am not a crook." It was a surreal time, indelible in my memory.

NIXON DEFIANT

"Contrition is BS. This President has nothing to apologize for. This President will not grovel to the American people." Ronald Ziegler, the staffer closest to an embattled Richard Nixon in his darkest hour, glowered at me and barked angrily.

I couldn't believe my ears, but I kept scribbling notes as Ziegler warmed to his theme. There was still a job to do, though it had just gotten much harder in the few minutes since I'd walked across the West Wing lobby from the national security adviser's office to meet with my former boss, the White House press secretary.

It was August 1973. The full-length windows behind Ron's desk looked out past the huge elms and the iron fence toward the sleepiness of Pennsylvania Avenue on a summer afternoon. The elegant room near the Oval Office was familiar from the year I had spent as a press aide, before becoming Nixon's youngest speechwriter at 26 in January 1971. Also familiar were the press secretary's hot temper and fierce loyalty to the Boss. What shocked me was the bunker mentality revealed in Ziegler's defiant outburst—likely reflective of the President's own views—when I explained Henry Kissinger's recommendation for the nationally televised speech on Watergate that we were supposed to work on together.

Scandal had been howling through the Nixon White House at gale force since March. Fallout from the June 1972 arrest of wiretappers connected with the President's campaign in Democratic party offices at the Watergate building, dismissed by Ziegler at the time as "a third-rate burglary attempt," now reached the highest levels of the newly reelected administration.

Nixon's two top aides, chief of staff Bob Haldeman and domestic policy director John Ehrlichman, had been forced out in April. John Dean, the disgraced White House counsel, formerly my neighbor in the Executive Office Building, dominated headlines in June as the star witness for Sen. Sam Ervin's select committee investigating Watergate. Revelation of a secret taping system in the Oval Office had rocked Washington during those hearings.

July brought a pause in the storm. Nixon took refuge at his Western White House complex in San Clemente, California. But the refuge couldn't last. Kissinger made that clear when I asked him one sunny day, outside the double-wide modular structures that served for offices there on the bluffs above the Pacific, "Why does the President behave so evasively in all this, as if guilty? Why can't he show the country he's with the hounds, not the foxes?"

"He can't pretend to lead the chase," Henry growled in disgust. "He is *one* of the foxes." He said no more and I didn't ask. The details he might have in mind were not for my ears. I felt no curiosity, only helpless dread.

Now we were at least back in Washington and preparing to do something. The plan was for President Nixon to go on TV with a candid, tell-all speech that would finally "put Watergate behind us." The address was set for the evening of August 15. Word came to chief speechwriter Ray Price from the new chief of staff, Gen. Alexander Haig, that Andrews was to write the first draft based on themes that Kissinger and Ziegler would spell out.

Dr. K. urged upon me one theme: "Contrition." Say that on the roof of your mouth, swallowing the "R," and you'll hear how it sounded in his famous German accent. Those three guttural syllables will echo with me always. Not only was Henry persuasive that afternoon (he was always persuasive); his approach intrinsically made sense to me.

The American people want to think well of their President, he pointed out. They are willing to forgive their President at a time like this. They are eager to. He only has to ask for it—but he must ask. Look at John F. Kennedy after the Bay of Pigs, Kissinger said. He shouldered the responsibility, accepted blame, showed contrition, and actually rose in public esteem as a result. Now was the time for Nixon to face the music as his old rival, JFK, had done, and reap similar goodwill. But the key was contrition.

Such were the notes that I read from my yellow pad to the frowning Ziegler, only to have him snort, "Contrition is BS." (He didn't use the abbreviation.) Ron continued with a pitch-perfect recitation of the Nixonian defensiveness, evasions, bluster, blaming, and victim talk that he believed would make for a better speech than the "groveling" approach Kissinger had suggested.

Glumly I jotted it all down and walked back to my office dejected. Bill Safire, my senior colleague on the writing staff, liked to tell of Franklin Roosevelt giving his speechwriter a high-tariff draft from

Commerce and a low-tariff draft from Treasury, of which the poor man was directed to make one speech. That was funny; this wasn't. There was no reconciling defiance and remorse. "Putting Watergate behind us" wouldn't happen any time soon.

The speech draft I finally submitted, a Kissinger-style plea for forgiveness, went nowhere. Nixon's Watergate report to the nation on August 15, 1973, instead took the spin that Ziegler, his alter ego, had called for. It accomplished nothing. Next came the cynically named Operation Candor, which only deepened the distrust hanging over the White House.

Nixon: Anything but contrite

The scandal would drag on for another full year. Its final act was the President's resignation on August 8, 1974, and his pardon by Gerald Ford a month later, both events unprecedented in American history. I was already gone from the White House by then, having quit with a public protest at the end of 1973.

DUTY DISOWNED

Could a different speech have saved Richard Nixon's presidency? No one can say, but I very much doubt it. Was young John Andrews capable of crafting such a feat of oratory in any case? Maybe, but again probably not.

Did the presidential unindicted co-conspirator even deserve to survive in office? Maybe not. Maybe Ford, his appointed successor, was right in saying, "The system worked." Or maybe it would have been better for the country, and more just to the man himself, if Nixon had outfoxed the hounds, hung on and beaten impeachment as Bill Clinton was later to do. While these things make interesting speculation, settling them is not my purpose here.

I tell the contrition story for a different reason. It takes us back 40 years to the unforgettable convergence of a defining moment in my life and a searing moment in America's story. It was a time when great forces in the rise and fall of nations seemed visible in daily events, rather than unseen below the surface—and those forces were moving ominously against the United States, even as the bicentennial of our independence approached.

How did Americans stem the onrushing tide of decline and then reverse it? What have I learned from carrying a musket, dodging bullets, and returning fire in in the ongoing battle of ideas from then to now? That's the story we'll explore in this book.

Everyone thinks of the 1960s as a period of turmoil, conflict, and seismic change in American life, and so it was. It was the 1970s, though, that saw the worst of the downhill slide into military, political, economic, social, cultural, and moral disarray which led some observers to conclude our best days were behind us.

From leaders like Jimmy Carter, and from groups like the Club of Rome with its pessimistic *Limits to Growth* report, came the verdict that America's time in the sun was over. We simply needed to accept our diminished status and reduced prospects and get used to it, this view went.

Vast impersonal causes beyond anyone's control had brought us to this, many believed. The United States had had a good run, but civilizational old age was catching up with her, just at the two-century mark as historians foresaw. Now it would be someone else's turn.

Not everyone agreed, however. The reasons for our troubles were neither mysterious nor inevitable, some voices insisted. What had brought us low was a widespread, persistent, worsening dereliction of duty by too many individuals and too many institutions throughout the land. The problem was a massive abdication of responsibility.

Doing your duty, fulfilling your trust, and expecting more of yourself than others—these obligations were once as much a constant in our way of life as twice-two-makes-four. Now the responsibility ethic had come to be seen as old-fashioned. In the jaded '70s it was finally shrugged off as completely passé. Duty? Who believes in that any more?

What a grim decade it was: Defeat in Vietnam, genocide in Cambodia, retreat before the Soviets on three continents, the Presidency dishonored, the armed services and intelligence agencies discredited, OPEC and oil shocks, the Panama Canal signed away, Castro's foreign adventurism, Arafat emboldened, Tehran hostages and the humiliation of Desert One, welfare out of control, crime rampant, epidemics of abortion and divorce, churches and universities demoralized, government metastasizing, economic stagflation with trade deficits and budget deficits.

SOME STOOD UP

But the worst deficit, the rottenness at the root in those years, was America's *responsibility deficit*. Thank goodness there were millions of citizens who realized that, deplored it, and resolved to stand against it. They were, to use an old-fashioned term, the remnant of the Republic.[7] Neither the root cause, epidemic irresponsibility, nor its symptom, national decline, was something they would take sitting down.

The remnant were no more prepared to accept that ours was a setting and not a rising sun than Benjamin Franklin had been at the Constitutional Convention of 1787.[8] They weren't about to give up on our country's founding principles just because the Kremlin proclaimed a Brezhnev Doctrine, or some judges launched a holocaust of the unborn, or the White House diagnosed us with malaise.

There was no quit in these stubborn middle Americans. At some point during the gloomy Carter years they began to turn and fight. Their numbers grew and their cause started to seem less impossible. I was one of them. You probably were too. They—we—gradually became the responsibility movement of this generation.

The rise of the remnant was felt as a political phenomenon, to be sure—a new force symbolized by names like Reagan and Gingrich— but it was also much more than that. Its impact has been felt economically, socially, and culturally as well. It has sometimes worked through the Republican and Democratic parties. At other times its gains have come in spite of one or both political parties.

One benefit from the rebirth of responsibility, unforeseeable when the elites believed we were washed up after Vietnam, was victory in the Cold War, the Gulf, and now Iraq. Another result has been reduction of pathologies like crime, drugs, abortion, racism. Others: welfare reform, long booms and shallow recessions, spectacular environmental gains.[9]

Life is still no rose garden for the USA, as joblessness and financial woes continue tormenting the economy. But we're a far stronger and more confident nation today than when irresponsibility was hitting bottom in the 1970s. The declinist obituaries for Uncle Sam were premature. The responsible remnant gets much of the credit.

HOW BRIGHT IS THE FUTURE?

In the coming chapters, we will trace responsibility's rebirth in the past generation and draw lessons for the next generation. We'll see how responsible America has reasserted itself and can sustain the reassertion, positioning the United States for continued world leadership in the next American century—the era to 2076 and beyond. We'll also take some case studies from my own experiences as a citizen in politics, five eventful decades from Sputnik and Little Rock to the 9/11 attacks and the Age of Obama.

Several debatable points arise with this approach:

- Betrayal of responsibility was clearly fatal in the slow-motion political suicide of President Nixon and his men between 1972 and 1974, as my contrition story typifies. But how well does this notion of a responsibility deficit explain our country's broader comedown from the pinnacle of power on VJ-Day in 1945 to the humiliation of helicopters evacuating Saigon in 1975?

- How essential was the rebirth of responsibility in rallying the American spirit since then? Has there been a serious, grownup shift of attitudes and values? Or was it merely a run of luck and a mood change?

- Beyond all that, how real is the bright future I foresee? Is the reader merely being romanced by Andrews the Pollyanna? Or conned by John the Paragon, one more politico peddling a memoir of "Do as I say, not as I do?"

Those answers are for you to decide. The author owns responsibility for a thorough examination of each point, and for honest self-scrutiny. The first step is to agree on a definition of responsibility, and to recognize its high place in the constellation of values that Americans have cherished from earliest times.

CHAPTER 3

RESPONSIBILITY
SUSTAINS FREEDOM

Ecclesiastes 9:14, 15

This love letter from a passionate American originated in the back of my mind long ago. I have a file cabinet full of half-begun outlines to prove it. But life only got me ready to write the book in my 60s, and it's a good thing.

Until quite recently, my keynote for a personal testament and a reflection on citizenship would not have been responsibility and obligation, duty and trust. It would have been freedom and independence, rights and liberty.

"Freedom is the master value." So I wrote in 1995 when spelling out a credo for *Andrews' America*, the little monthly I used to publish.[10] And freedom has in fact been a guiding star of my political life from college days onward.

Yet in reflecting on my life as a whole—family, friendships, schooling, military service, career, community, church—I've realized that most of it was not about doing what I chose, but doing what I should. The moral and ethical component is inescapable in a life well lived, whether for an individual or a nation.

Duty is nearer to each of us than our own skin. Obligations and gratitude to others were debited against my account and yours, humanly and spiritually, before we ever walked or talked. You may accept this as an obvious reality, or you may resist it as an imposition on your sense of personal autonomy. Generationally, millennials are apt to discount this ethic of obligation and gratitude. The contagion of selfishness and entitlement has infected too many of them. But if you think honestly about your own life—even if you don't happen to hold a religious faith—you will reach the same conclusion I have. If you study history, you will reach the same conclusion I have.

A LAW LIKE GRAVITY

Responsibility, I'll venture to say, is a law. Or if you prefer, it's an element or force, something like oxygen or gravity, foundational and undeniable. We can ignore the element of responsibility at our peril, or embrace it to our profit. What we cannot do is evade it without consequences.

Endeavoring to act as we should, with self-knowledge that the obligation exists, is the essence of being human. The moral consciousness of "I should, you should" enlightens no other living thing but you and me, the sons and daughters of Adam and Eve. Now take the reasoning a step further; and here I expect disagreement:

This book will argue that the essence of being an American is a life of acting as we should, with wide self-determination as to what the obligation means.

It's true that no country ever envisioned such unlimited possibilities for itself and its citizens as ours does. But no country has ever expected so much of itself and its citizens as America does either.

As a nation we are defined by responsibility and freedom inseparably joined—with responsibility as the senior partner, the tiebreaker. *May* and *ought* exist together or not at all—and *ought* comes first. Responsibility enables freedom. Our revolution as specifically chartered on July 4, 1776, sprang from this understanding.

America's birth certificate in the Declaration of Independence, "all created equal and endowed with unalienable rights," indeed proclaims liberty. But it does so only after acknowledging the higher "laws of nature and of nature's God," along with the neighborly obligation of "a decent respect to the opinions of mankind."[11]

Responsibility breathes in every sentence of the Declaration. There was a right order of things, natural, fitting, and just, a moral horizon which these Founders discerned as clearly as I can see the ridge of the Rockies out my window today—and wherein they acted as trustees and agents to bring forth the new nation.

We are doing what is "necessary," Jefferson and his colleagues assert in the opening line. We are responding to a "necessity which constrains" us, they repeat a few lines later. "We must acquiesce in the necessity," they say again near the close.

"Their right, their duty," separated only by a comma and virtually synonymous, appear at the climax of the Declaration's second paragraph. The Americans felt themselves answerable to an ultimate imperative, a mighty obligation. They were seizing nationhood not simply because they chose, but because they must. How utterly opposite from the relativistic worldview of more recent times.

No irresponsible rebels, they had carried loyalty, obedience, and prudence to the breaking point. Their "most humble terms" addressed from subjects to monarch had only shown him "unfit to be the ruler of a free people." Their brotherly "attention… to our common kindred" had found the mother country "deaf to the voice of justice."

Other appeals being exhausted, "the Supreme Judge of the world" must finally hear their case. "A candid world" could not fail to see that the united colonies "ought to be" independent states. Connection with Britain "ought to be" totally dissolved. To make it so, the signers pledged conscience and blood, "sacred honor" and a steely willingness to die if need be.

HARDWIRED

Any honest reading of the state papers, pamphlets, sermons and letters of the colonial and revolutionary periods will yield the same conclusion as this brief review: Responsibility is hardwired into the American character. It's in our DNA as "one people assum[ing] among the powers of the earth [our] separate and equal station."

From long before 1776, the self-understanding of the American polity has rested upon unequivocal truths about how a political order *should* treat its members and how those members *should* treat each other. Even in the 1630s when pilgrim settlers aspired to be a "city on a hill," in the biblical words invoked by Governor John Winthrop and latterly by President Ronald Reagan, it was not so individuals could boast from the top of that hill or soar off it Icarus-fashion.[12] The idea was that from up there we would *serve* together for all nations as an example of righteousness and a beacon of rescue.

Our heritage of moral duty puts to shame the laziness, shallowness, and selfishness of contemporary intellectual fashion. It exposes the corrosive amorality and solipsism summed up in a Supreme Court decision claiming that "at the heart of liberty is the right to define one's own concept of existence, of meaning, of the universe, and of the mystery of human life."[13]

The honorable Justices could not have been more wrong. In these United States, the truth is that still today as forever in centuries past, responsibility—seeing our way, each on his own as far as good order allows, to what must be obeyed, and then obeying it, by voluntary choice as far as the common weal can tolerate—underlies freedom and takes precedence before freedom.

AMERICA'S TREASURE

Responsibility is an inescapable element in the life of *any* person or nation. But so central is responsibility to the American founding and identity that it stands as the uniquely treasured heritage of our country in particular. This is not less true even amidst today's lax mores where irresponsible indulgence is accepted and celebrated.

For this American, then, it's no longer freedom that is the master value. It is freedom's obverse, responsibility. My dawning awareness of this over the past decade has come with the tempering one acquires in becoming a grandfather, a senator (literally, "an elder"), and a Christian convert.

Arresting and disturbing was the confession of one of my fathers in Christ, C. S. Lewis, who demurred: "I was not born to be free. I was born to adore and obey."[14] Those words constantly chasten me.

Further chastening came as I watched Donna attending to her dying mother at one moment—and to our toddler grandson a moment later. The mutual self-giving and sacrifices of a family across the generations express a richness of responsibility undreamt of in the pure libertarian ethic of self-assertion and self-reliance alone.

Even in the political realm, working to enact a freedom agenda in the Colorado Senate, I realized how greatly our proposals and votes were dependent on the constitution to which we all swore, the statutes that bound us, and the rules we worked under, not to mention the unwritten code imposed us by faith and flag. As legislators, in other words, doing what we should was the iron precondition for doing what we chose.

Two personal heroes also helped me recognize responsibility as America's treasure. One was Dr. Guy McBride, president emeritus of the Colorado School of Mines, who recruited me to teach politics there. The other was Prof. Harry Jaffa, grand old man of the Claremont Institute, whose noble example inspirits that organization where I worked after leaving the Senate.

My years of imbibing Claremont's vindication of the Founders and Lincoln, along with countless hours of thinking with honor students at the School of Mines about how freedom and obligation are paradoxically joined, prepared me invaluably for writing this book.

When the book finally emerged, therefore, it became more a reflection on responsibility than a rallying cry for liberty. It became, in addition, an exploration of what America means—not just a recitation of what conservatism teaches and proposes.

BEYOND RIGHT AND LEFT

Why the shift? Some would have said the Andrews conservative manifesto was a natural. It seemed ordained by my formative years in the 1960s and '70s, when I devoured Goldwater's *Conscience of a Conservative* in high school, supported his presidential campaign in college and thrilled to Reagan's role in it, defended the Vietnam War in national magazines, and wrote for Bill Buckley's *National Review*.

It would logically cap all my work from the '80s to the present, one might think—a journey with stops at Hillsdale College, the Independence Institute, State Policy Network, TCI Cable News, Backbone Radio, Claremont Institute, and Centennial Institute, punctuated by campaigns seeking to keep Colorado in the Republican column and move it rightward.

Let there be no doubt: I am inexpressibly grateful for that long eventful road. I remain as committed a conservative as you'll find. But in lieu of "one more conservative book for the faithful," I feel urgency for this idea of responsibility as America's defining heritage, responsibility reborn in our generation, and responsibility as a key to the next century.

Our toughest challenges now are not political. They are moral. Civil government will get better when individual self-government does, and not until then. That was always the deepest insight of the conservative movement. Its loss has led to conservatism's faltering drive and fragmenting factions in this decade. The movement has become a shadow of its former self, static and stale. I have no fix-it plan other than a summons back to basics—American basics, not ideological basics.

The ideal that I call responsible America is what the conservative movement originally set out to conserve. The remnant sensed a growing amnesia about our very identity as a people. Approaching 1976, there was an impetus to renew the spirit of 1776. What moved the movement was a concern that all Americans together—right, left, and center—needed to lift our sights again to the city on a hill and leave the swamps of self-indulgence.

In those Ford and Carter years, many realized that America's future was looking more and more like Europe's. Ennui and enervation, selfishness and secularism, multicultural relativism, hope yielding to resignation, the ethos of anything goes and "whatever," began to define the USA. How could such alien attitudes so quickly displace the idealism and sacrifice that Americans had carried overseas in uniform only a generation before? This couldn't possibly be our destiny.

We were and must remain the New World. Americans had always understood that while the European past had given us much to cherish, the European future led in a direction we did not want to go.

We knew this in breaking from old Europe in the 1700s; again in resisting Europe's encroachment during the 1800s while welcoming their unwanted poor; and yet again in saving Europe from tyranny three times in the 1900s while claiming no land but cemeteries for our dead. We knew now, that the slide into Old World entropy had to stop.

With the alarm of someone fighting a heart attack, elements throughout American society awoke to resist. Tough-mindedness spread. The conservative political movement was one result, but not the only one. The awakening was also felt on the social and cultural, economic and educational, moral and spiritual fronts—not just in the voting booth and the halls of government but everywhere from the boardroom to the classroom to the sickroom.

Overall, this trend of the past three decades I believe is really best described as a *responsibility movement*. The movement—if such it is, a proposition I will undertake to prove—has been largely unconscious of itself as such. But it has been, I contend, all the more powerful for that very reason. Its common-sense persistence and pervasiveness have again and again transcended partisan politics and election cycles. Doubt this? Stay with me and see if I make my case.

AN EXPERIMENT

It is because I believe in the surpassing importance of this unnoticed elemental force, Element R, invisible but inexorable, that I am determined not to write in conservative-speak. It seems to me there is simply a better way to think about our country's recent past and near future. This is frankly an experiment. There may be nothing else like it. So let's give this a try.

Political labels are problematic these days, in any case. Their accuracy is questionable, and their usefulness in campaigns seems to be on the wane. Opponents' efforts in 2008 to tag Barack Obama as a "leftist" or "socialist," and Mark Udall as a "Boulder liberal" in his US Senate race from Colorado, didn't keep either man from winning easily.

Label-slinging and spectrum-splitting is a political insiders' waste of time. Republicans talking up how conservative they are, often as a substitute for simply proving it while speaking plain English, have given such talk a bad name. Let others play those games. I'm not interested in debating how many angels can dance on the head of a pollster.

Matters get further confused when icons like Friedrich Hayek, the great economist and philosopher of liberty, identify themselves as liberals (or sometimes "classical liberals") in the 19th-century tradition of John Stuart Mill, Frederic Bastiat, and Lord Acton. Hayek not only helped found modern conservatism with his 1946 book, *The Road to Serfdom*. He also published the famous essay, "Why I am Not a Conservative."

NOVUS ORDO SECLORUM

What about the Founders? Were they conservatives? My side of the aisle insists they were. Yet a revolution, by its very nature, is not easy for conservatives to come to terms with. Breaking with the past, and violently so, seems irreconcilable with the conserving impulse. It might appear that today's innovators, the liberals and progressives, have as good a claim—or better—on our nation's origins than the traditionalists of the right.

What if the jealous siblings could be shown to be joint heirs? Might the recognition of a common heritage help us to a common purpose? At the very least, it could encourage a more amicable and less polarized approach to current contentions. A recent book by William B. Allen casts George Washington, of all people, as "America's first progressive."[15] Though writing as a conservative, Allen challenges both sides to rethink our categories and assumptions. We need to.

You can make a strong case that the United States was born not with an ideological vector to either the right or the left—but with a moral instinct *upward* to the way human communities were meant to be. "We have it in our power to begin the world anew," wrote Thomas Paine. Actually they neither had the power nor made the attempt—it was the revolutionaries in France who disastrously did that—but such was the mood of the time.

Look at the Great Seal on the back of a dollar bill. *Novus Ordo Seclorum*, it says: "A new order of the ages." We see a pyramid, partly built, under God's all-seeing eye. The idea is aspiration and imagination tempered with discipline and diligence, audacious yet accountable to authority. An eternal standard is implied.

This is one more example, small but telling, of my argument that responsibility, doing what we should, is at the very heart of America's origins. Other familiar examples span those early centuries, starting before the War of Independence and continuing well after. There were the stern words of duty at Jamestown and Plymouth Rock; from Jonathan Edwards in the pulpit; from Poor Richard with his almanac. There was the virtue of John and Abigail Adams in Boston, the nobility of George Washington declining a kingship and creating the presidency.

There were Hamilton, Jay, and Madison penning their masterpiece of principle and prudence, *The Federalist*. Across the Atlantic there was Adam Smith, preaching character in *The Theory of Moral Sentiments* as a counterweight to acquisitiveness in *The Wealth of Nations*. There were Jefferson and Adams, once the bitterest of enemies, exchanging enmity for friendship in old age, reconciled by their shared abhorrence of slavery and dread of disunion.

Up, strive, be better, try harder, yield not, do right. That's the ethic in which responsible America originated. Having rights was only part of it. *Doing* right was the other part, the cornerstone of the pyramid. The "Supreme Judge of the World" is ever watching as humans build and plant, declare and found, fight and legislate. There is a plumbline. Responsibility enables freedom.

The upward vector for American renewal was identified by Ronald Reagan in his famous "Time for Choosing" speech on October 27, 1964. "There is no such thing as a left or right," said Reagan on national television in support of Barry Goldwater's presidential candidacy. "There is only an up or down—up to man's age-old dream, the ultimate in individual freedom consistent with law and order—or down to the ant heap of totalitarianism."[16] Alexander Solzhenitsyn, the great voice of conscience against Soviet tyranny, would invoke a similar image in his Harvard address a dozen years later.

Fresh perspectives emerge when we think about the last century and the next one in terms of responsibility vs. irresponsibility, for a change from the endlessly debated polarization of right vs. left. It

Reagan: Upward vector

seems to me that the resisters whom I've called the remnant instinctively drew upon this foundational sense of character from our country's beginnings in the 1770s to counter the cultural chaos of the 1970s—the nihilism of "do your own thing, anything goes."

Burnt-out and beaten down as we seemed, a flame of purpose still lit the way upward for our institutions and aspirations to revive. The remnant knew what the Founders knew. Exhausted America had not lost its moral core.

Nor had Americans lost their awareness of a high calling in history, the sense of exceptionalism as an "almost-chosen people," in Lincoln's phrase. Rejecting the "come home" defeatism of George McGovern, which President Nixon warned was code for "acid, amnesty, and abortion," they gave the unlovable incumbent 49 states in November 1972. Then twenty-one months later they rejected Nixon in turn, disgusted by his Watergate "breach of faith," as Theodore White put it in a book by that title.[17]

Right and left didn't have a lot to do with it. Our country was simply better than this, the Founders would have said, and the silent majority knew it. When Goldwater led a Senate delegation to the White House, the unindicted presidential co-conspirator knew it too. As he helicoptered off to exile in San Clemente, responsibility's rebirth was beginning to gestate.

CHAPTER 4

NOT A SETTING SUN

Daniel 2:20, 21

"The average age of the world's greatest civilizations from the beginning of history has been about 200 years," an historian has concluded. "Every democracy will finally collapse due to loose fiscal policy," he warns. As Americans living in a country now well into its third century and facing trillion-dollar deficits, we have to be sobered by these words. They are attributed to Alexander Tytler, a scholar at the University of Edinburgh in the late 18th century.

In Philadelphia at about the same period, Benjamin Franklin encouraged the Constitutional Convention to believe that the solar motif carved in the president's chair, where George Washington sat, represented America's bright prospects with "a rising and not a setting sun."[18] But here was a learned Scot, Tytler, the contemporary and countryman of Adam Smith, pronouncing sharply to the contrary about what the young republic's future might hold.

What is the relevance of his warning for the time frame of our discussion here: the 1976 bicentennial period, the Age of Obama today, and the far horizon of 2076? Is sundown overtaking us? Or does "morning in America," proclaimed by the ever-optimistic President Reagan, still prevail?

WARNINGS OF DECLINE

The Enlightenment's Alexander Tytler and and his modern counterpart, John Glubb, are the contrarians looking on skeptically as we trace the rebirth of responsibility in recent years and seek its continuation going forward. These two are not the only writers who suggest that according to the cycles of history, the United States has probably had its day and there is little we can do. But they are set apart by an emphasis on character and the moral dimension.

Though Tytler's books are seldom read today, a quotation cited to him has gained fame through speeches and radio, articles and the Web. Doesn't this have the ring of truth?

> The average age of the world's greatest civilizations from the beginning of history has been about 200 years. During those 200 years, those nations always progressed through the following sequence: from bondage to spiritual faith, from spiritual faith to great courage, from courage to liberty, from liberty to abundance, from abundance to complacency, from complacency to apathy, from apathy to dependence, and from dependence back into bondage.

The 200-year time span might be debated. But there is immediate persuasiveness in the moral and material trajectory described here, from the depths of dependence and bondage to the heights of liberty and abundance, then back down again. You'd have to be dreaming, not to recognize that we live in a nation that has for quite a while been somewhere on the declining side of the cycle. Of course a trend is not necessarily irreversible, and a pattern isn't destiny. "I show you things that could be," said the ghost to Scrooge, "not things that will be."

But what is it about abundance that breeds complacency? Does dependence always follow from apathy? Is bondage really anything to worry about in the humane and enlightened world of today? What are the signs that any one stage of decline is overtaking a nation and worsening toward the next stage? How can those who sense the danger intervene to reignite faith and courage? Where in the sequence was America a hundred years ago? Thirty years ago? Today?

We need to be asking ourselves these questions —even if the warning did not originate with Tytler, as literary detectives now suspect.[19] Wisdom is no less wise for being apocryphal, if the shoe fits.

This appraisal fits our situation uncomfortably well, whatever its origin. Let's call it the Tytler analysis for convenience, much as Dickens called his messenger the ghost, and proceed to the substance of the matter. There is further substance to concern us. Prior to stating the 200-year cycle, the same passage warns:

> A democracy is always temporary in nature; it simply cannot exist as a permanent form of government. A democracy will continue to exist up until the time that voters discover they can vote themselves generous gifts from the public treasury. From that moment on, the majority always vote for the candidates who promise the most benefits from the public treasury, with the result that every democracy will finally collapse due to loose fiscal policy, which is always followed by a dictatorship.

Fitting indeed, one would have to conclude after the recent economic upheavals in America and Europe alike. While dictatorship is not yet talked of, the autumn of 2008 did see the U. S. Secretary of the Treasury, a *Republican,* request and receive the most sweeping powers over our economy that any individual has ever held. The accession of a Democratic President and an enlarged Democratic Congress in 2009 made it possible for those powers and other massive expansions of government, blamed on the financial crisis, to aggrandize even further. The substantial gains made by Republicans in the 2010 election will not soon undo the damage, even if they slow the trend.

Endless budget deficits and borrowing, debasement of the currency, unsustainable entitlement programs, public benefits as a magnet for illegal immigration across undefended borders, and an ever larger proportion of the American people excused from the tax rolls—these factors have steadily eroded responsibility just as the Tytler analysis warns. On top of all that, the politically-driven mortgage bubble, set off by social-engineering, constituency-bribing operators at Fannie

Mae and Freddie Mac, finally brought the crash that grim-faced historians had foreseen.

Under Obama, command and control are making their greatest inroads against capitalism and consent in American life since Franklin Roosevelt's time. "Democracy will collapse due to loose fiscal policy," the analysis predicts. Somewhere Alexander Tytler, or the anonymous oracle who channeled him, is shaking his head sadly. Whoever he is, he told us so.

TEN GENERATIONS

All is not well in the city on a hill, to say the least. Liberty is already a casualty and abundance is imperiled. Some sense the quickening descent toward dependence. The Tea Party phenomenon is a wakeup call against complacency and apathy. But dependence was apparently not a concern to the millions who voted to put Obama in the White House.

Indeed there are signs that many see dependence coming and welcome it. There is in this country today, as in every country at every period, an element that ignores or actively disclaims responsibility. Even with the Tea Party pushing back, these irresponsibles have more weight right now than at any time since McGovern and Carter. We have to hope that Element R, the responsible remnant that has already brought us so far, will set a counter-example and stand against them in the public arena.

Complacency to apathy to dependence to bondage, Tytler's toppling dominoes of self-defeat, may have already begun to fall in America's third century. Arguably things are getting away from us, with blame to go around for left and right alike. The late Sir John Glubb (1897-1986), if he were still here observing the scene, would be saddened but not surprised. Yet I believe he would also have a realistic word of hope.

Who was Glubb? He published 17 books after a notable military career that began in the British Army and ended with two decades as commander of Jordan's Arab Legion. In a slender work called *The Fate of Empires*, written the very year of America's bicentennial, he advanced a cyclical theory similar to the one attributed to Tytler (whom he does not cite), but more fully argued. Taking a dozen instances from ancient and modern times, Glubb summarizes:

> In a surprising manner, 250 years emerges as the average length of national greatness. This average has not varied for 3,000 years. Does it represent ten generations? The stages of the rise and fall of great nations seem to be: the age of pioneers, the age of conquests, the age of commerce, the age of affluence, the age of intellect, and the age of decadence. Decadence is marked by defensiveness, pessimism, materialism, frivolity, an influx of foreigners, the welfare state, and the weakening of religion. Decadence is due to too long a period of wealth and power, selfishness, love of money, and the loss of a sense of duty. [20]

Frivolity? Selfishness? Loss of a sense of duty? The portrait would seem equally applicable to the last days of Rome and the last days of disco. A responsibility deficit dominated both. From Assyria and Persia eons ago to the British and American experience today, Glubb writes, the "high noon" of the nation is in its periods of conquest, commerce, and affluence. But even then, beneath the surface, gradually comes "the change... from service to selfishness," the creeping symptoms of irresponsibility.[21] Glubb dates the onset of America's afternoon sometime before 1920.

Although wonderful advances in education and science illumine the age of intellect, says Glubb, their "dangerous by-product... is the unconscious growth of the idea that the human brain can solve the problems of the world." Politically this leads to "an unceasing cacophony of argument [which] seems to destroy the power of action. Amid a Babel of talk, the ship drifts onto the rocks." [22]

Bottom line: "The impression that the situation can be saved by mental cleverness, without unselfishness or human self-dedication, can only lead to collapse."[23] The parallels to our circumstances in this country today are too obvious to require spelling out. Yet Glubb acknowledges that the future remains in our hands.

With an informed public, he speculates, the UK or the US might still shake off demoralization through policies "to maintain the spirit of duty and self-sacrifice… and the initiative needed to give rise to action."[24] This was in 1978. Thatcher and Reagan were in the wings. Element R was gathering strength in both countries. The trend of things has improved notably since then, though great challenges remain. The ledger is not yet closed on either nation.

Margaret Thatcher roused the UK

Sir John's 250 years from the age of pioneers to the depths of decadence, slightly longer than the 200 years posited by "Tytler," correlate to ten generations at 25 years each. My son and daughters, born in the Vietnam years, are of the tenth generation since the American Founders. Barack Obama and Sarah Palin, born a bit earlier, fit in the same cohort. John McCain and Joe Biden, my older contemporaries, would be in the ninth generation.

These things are inexact, of course, but there is no avoiding the point: According to the repetitive story of great nations since before Moses and Homer, time is running out for the almost-chosen people and their *Novus Ordo Seclorum*. Implacable enemies and impatient rivals are out there. Islam is afire. China is rising. If we coast, we're toast. If we exert ourselves, though, the story may be different this time. There is no law that says the United States of America can't break the cycle.

WHAT WE CAN DO

Glubb devoted the last part of *The Fate of Empires* to a discussion of issues raised by readers of his original magazine article from which the book grew. The article's purpose, he stressed, was not to suggest fatalistically that "the end is nigh," but rather to insist "we can save ourselves." He was sure of it. His concluding agenda in the book, a summons to responsibility with 22 action points, says in part:

Every one of us can contribute to the recovery of our country by working harder and by fostering a sense of comradeship and teamwork.... Love, patient and benevolent, will always find a way.... Only a revival of spiritual devotion, not fashionable "isms," can inspire selfless service.... Each one of us can contribute by leading moral and dedicated lives.... If we have no leaders to inspire us, we must "go it alone." [25]

Have you ever felt you were going it alone? I have. But in Sir John Glubb, stern and somber as he may be, we find one of those leaders who can inspire us—and reconnect us. You will meet others in these pages. I have spent a lifetime looking for such leaders, following them, and seeking to emulate them as a leader myself in the battle of ideas and the battle of votes, the battle for a responsible America. From those experiences came this book.

Heroes and mentors, starting with my father and uncles, showed me it is truly possible to live up to Sir John's challenge. They translated responsibility from the theoretical to the practical in the crucible of daily duty. Millions who quietly do their duty each day, a few of them with famous names but most known only to neighbors and family, comprise the responsible remnant. I am grateful to be a small imperfect part of it.

If I am right about the rebirth of responsibility—which began three decades ago in a dark time for our nation, has already brought us far, and is still today (at another difficult time) gaining strength across America, reconnecting us with our founding principles, renewing civil society, and preparing us for world leadership in the new century—we are not going to be the late great USA at the 250-year mark.

If I am right, it's not going to be tough luck, ten generations and out, for my grandson Ian and his grade-school classmates. Responsibility reborn will mean that Franklin's sun is still on the rise and America's best days are ahead. This *will* be the next American century. So let's see if I'm right.

PART TWO

LESSONS

CHAPTER 5

THE KID FROM BACKBONE

Exodus 20:12

L ike any other love letter, this paean to responsible America is
partly description and partly aspiration. The lover knows what
he is and what the beloved is. He also knows what he and the beloved
may both become. He is mindful, or tries to be, of how they may
both fall short, certainly now and probably in the future, perhaps
always.

"Responsible America" is like a Homeric epithet or a title of
honor. Crafty Odysseus didn't always measure up to his name, nor
was Frederick the Great a great hero to his valet. The epithet captures
essence and potentiality. It's not a claim of static perfection. There is
allowance for seasons and stumbles, times of eclipse, the realities of
a fallen world.

So America and all of us as Americans will not always be found
faithful to our national treasure, the responsibility ethic. Earlier we
took a panoramic sketch of the nation's time of eclipse. We looked at
how much leeway the cyclical ideas of Tytler and Glubb might allow
for responsible America's renewal. Sir John certainly granted the possibility. "We can save ourselves," he challenged.[26]

One by one is the only way, however. Laws and bureaucracies are
not the answer. Responsibility is inescapably personal. Glubb again:
"Every one of us can contribute to the recovery of our country by

working harder and by fostering a sense of comradeship and team-work… by leading moral and dedicated lives."[27] (Footnote 26) To see what that might look like, we'll now take a closeup of a single American life—mine.

Not because I am extraordinary, but precisely because I'm quite ordinary, this may help illumine where America has been and where it can go. Could it be that all of us, whatever our imperfections, are constantly pulled to be better by *the responsible core of what America is*, like a magnetic field pulling the compass needle to north? My lessons and experiences suggest it is so.

COWBOY BRIGADOON

I was born near the lakeshore in the orchards of western Michigan among my mother's family, the Hutchinsons. We soon moved to St. Louis, Missouri, so I could attend a school for Christian Scientists that my Andrews grandparents had helped establish. In 1955, the summer I was 11, life changed with a bang when my dad gambled on starting a boys' camp in the Collegiate Peaks region of Colorado.

It was a die-and-go-to-heaven experience for me and my brother Jim, two years younger. For the next few years, everything else in my world was just filler until early June, when we'd all pile in the station wagon, trek across Kansas, and prepare to welcome campers from all over the country to Sky Valley Ranch in the shadow of Mount Yale and Mount Princeton.

Hiking to the top of those peaks, 14,000 feet above sea level, stirred my spirit like nothing else. My mother liked to quote the naturalist John Muir about how a mountain day can "open a thousand windows to show us God," and I have always found it so.[28]

Sometimes by jeep or horseback we'd head for the ghost towns of Colorado's mining days, places like Garfield, Harvard City, or St. Elmo. If you believed Pete Smythe, the morning radio guy on KOA in Denver, there was one little spot called East Tincup where the old-timers were still kicking. He said it was way up Cottonwood Creek west of Buena Vista, almost to the Divide.

Actually the place existed only in Pete's wild imagination, a sort of cowboy Brigadoon. But its ghost stuck with me. Years later as a political leader in the 1990s, I began talking about an imaginary high-country town of my own: Backbone Colorado USA.

Backbone is my hometown of the heart, hard to find up there near timberline, but impossible to forget once you've been there. Its name derives from the spine of the American continent, the craggy, windswept watershed between Atlantic and Pacific that snakes across Colorado north to south on its way from Canada to Mexico.

Backbone's name also evokes the purpose and principles that give skeletal strength to human character, differentiating man from worm. And it harkens to the foundational truths from Scripture and Constitution that define America itself. For all those reasons it's a destination to conjure with.

What if there was really such a place, a community where people's lives embodied all those things—respect for each other, devotion to the good, love of the land, decency, dignity? And what if it was not just an escapist place you'd fantasize about, but a practical identity you could bring with you anywhere? Think of the difference that could make in our world.

The good news is that precisely because Backbone Colorado USA is made-up in the geographic sense, it *can* be real in the sense that matters most. Backbone is a real way of life wherever there is one individual with backbone. Backbone as a community is real, wherever there are two such individuals. So what are we waiting for? The backbone way of life can be ours here and now.

HOW THE CLASSROOM WORKS

"We think there's not enough backbone in politics today, and we're out to remedy that," I often say when people ask about my broadcasting and blogging under that name. This usually gets ready agreement.

Not that we achieved any magical consensus when I was Republican leader of the Colorado Senate, 2001-2005, two years leading the minority and two more as president. There were constant sharp differences with the other party over legislation and budgets, growing from our disagreement on the backbone fundamentals mentioned above: purposes and principles, Scripture and Constitution. There was no shortage of differences within my party either.

But my being known as "the Senator from Backbone" (though elected from a Denver suburb called Centennial) left no doubt with friend or foe about what I stood for. Such clarity is itself welcome amid the often-spineless politics of our times.

You can see the kinship between the idea of backbone and that of responsibility. They are two ways of talking about the same thing. I once thought of doing a whole book on my life-lessons about responsible America and naming it after the imaginary town up on the Divide—"Back to Backbone," or something like that. Bad idea, I decided; it sounded like the self-written press release of a guy who thought he had it all together and believed the whole country would too, if they'd just read *my* book.

No way—that's not the message here. Andrews does not exemplify the responsibility ethic. I haven't led a perfectly responsible life; far from it. The only perfectly responsible life known to history was the one Christ led. He's the Master. The rest of us, me emphatically, are but learners in the world's classroom, and slow learners at that. If my experiences in citizenship, civics, and politics have any place in a book like this one, it's simply as a case study in how the classroom works.

PARADOX OF SUCCESS

"Paradoxes of the Human Condition" was our topic for that freshman honors course I mentioned helping teach for 18 years at the Colorado School of Mines. One of those paradoxes, it seems to me, involves success and responsibility. It goes this way:

You can't have much success in any area of life without conducting yourself responsibly. Talent and luck may be part of it, but genuine achievement depends on hard work, dedication, planning, promises kept, consideration for others, honesty and honor, courage and persistence, self-discipline and self-correction, all the attributes that go to make up responsibility. The more success you have, though, the easier it is to let yourself believe that responsibility is optional. Behaving less responsibly becomes quite tempting, and this in turn puts your success at risk.

That's the paradox of success. Another aspect of the same paradox is the tough reality that living responsibly does not always translate into success, at least the kind of success that the world recognizes and people dream about. Trying to content yourself with responsibility as its own reward amidst a world dizzy with affluence and status is like having to eat tofu at a steakhouse.

Life is not fair, as President Kennedy said. Responsibility is a necessary but not sufficient condition for success. The paradox arises again when an individual or group, believing themselves unjustly denied success despite a responsible record, concludes responsibility is a cheat. Irresponsible behavior then puts success even further out of reach.

The world's classroom gradually teaches us either by observation or by suffering that the paradox is always there and that it will bite you if ignored. Responsibility is never optional. Nor is responsibility ever a cheat. But responsibility's rewards tend to be subtle and silent. They are often long in coming, and very easily overlooked.

Responsibility is most imperative precisely when it seems the least necessary or the least just. This is what the paradox of success insists we learn. Welcome to the school of hard knocks, the course no one skips. What lets us know our grade? There is seldom an explicit report card. Most of the time our "responsibility GPA" is implicit in the daily flow of life's results and relationships, going well or not so well.

We did sometimes give grades for people in the news on Backbone Radio, the Sunday evening show I used to do. "A through F, snap answers, no fudging, tell us how they performed," I would ask Matt Dunn and Krista Kafer, my cohosts. Never mind, for the moment, being gentle or nice; there's a world of accountability a coldly objective letter-grade.

That idea of a report card *on myself* is what I now want to explore in some detail. How clearly or quickly did John "get it" about the imperative of responsibility at various turning points over the years? Bright as I supposedly was, were there times when I flunked and needed a retake? Where did the seductions of success creep in? When did the paradox bite? Did frustration and self-pity sometimes seem to justify irresponsibility?

What finally is the "responsibility GPA" on a lucky and ambitious guy with most of life's road now behind him? More important still, what analogy can we draw between one slow-learning American of the Boomer Generation—the author—and America's own collective drama of responsibility and irresponsibility in these times?

The warnings of decline from Glubb and Tytler suggest that irresponsibility fed by success eventually besets all great nations. The USA in the century just ended may be a prime example. Could the report card on myself become a template for a report card on my country? It might.

HOOKED ON POLITICS

Getting straight A's can do funny things to a kid. So can walking around under the invisible halo of being the camp director's son all summer and the headmaster's nephew all winter. So, I guess, can being the oldest of four in a fairly well-off family, reasonably nice-looking, and if that weren't enough, forever first in the alphabet. I seldom suffered from a lack of confidence, and more often from the opposite.

Yet mine was a very normal 1950s boyhood in Michigan, Missouri, and Colorado. On report cards in those years, in addition to academic honors, I probably got good marks for "Assumes responsibility." In high school at Principia in St. Louis, being something of a natural leader, I was tapped for class president and later student body president. Track, soccer, and football were my passions athletically. I would have told you back then that my greatest hero was my father, John Kneeland Andrews, decorated for valor as a submarine officer in the Pacific war. Submarine duty became a goal of mine.

Grandfather George Andrews, a Naval Academy graduate who had become a history professor and dean of Principia College in Elsah, Illinois, took my brother and me on a Lincoln pilgrimage to nearby New Salem and Springfield. It was one of those days you never forget; I was about ten. In February the following year, Jim insisted we mark Lincoln's birthday by setting a candle and a portrait of him on the family dinner table. About that same period, Jim got to visit the Alamo with Dad on a trip to San Antonio. I vicariously lived the experience with them.

"What's a Conservative, What's a Liberal?" was the high school term paper I was proudest of. By senior year, 1962, I had had a glimpse of both Richard Nixon and Barry Goldwater while serving as a Republican National Convention page, and had eagerly read Goldwater's *The Conscience of Conservative*, given me by someone as a gift.[29] I don't remember who got me the book, but it probably wasn't my father and mother. They were both quite apolitical, despite Uncle Ed Hutchinson's political career back in Michigan. Anyway, by the time I entered Principia College as

Goldwater's book started it

a political science major, I was very much a young man of the right. Hooked.

When people ask how I got into politics, I say I didn't. Politics got into me, somewhere back in my teens, and that was it for life. The

Landmark Books, a young people's library of American history and heroes, had something to do with my political fascination. So did a number of unforgettable teachers, among them Dorothy Roman of Buena Vista (where I attended half of eighth grade), the widow of a White Russian who had fled the Bolsheviks in 1917. So did the Cold War urgency that gripped those Eisenhower and Kennedy years, intensifying every aspect of American politics for a kid like me.

GENTLEMAN'S C

Civic participation, instinctive patriotism, and common-sense conservatism seemed to be in the water everywhere I grew up. Faith, family, and freedom, indivisible and unquestionable, were the very air that Jim and I and Eleanor and Sally breathed as kids. Ours was truly a Backbone upbringing, a gift to us from our parents and relatives and the community they chose to be part of.

Yet it's not with faux humility that I persist in calling myself a slow learner on some of life's most important lessons. Top grades, school prizes, and check marks in the character column didn't tell the whole story about young "Johnnie A." (As I said, being an early standout can do odd things to a fellow, among them the bestowal of a cloying nickname.)

If we define personal responsibility as involving a levelheaded sense of who you are and aren't, along with a solid grasp of your obligations to others, I was moving toward adulthood with some serious gaps on the report card.

The criteria for "Assumes responsibility," when you unpack them a bit, might include such things as "Recognizes it's not all about him"… "Practices self-criticism and self-correction"… "Shows consideration for other people"… and "Consistently distinguishes reality from fantasy." My youthful successes put the paradox in play for habits and skills such as these. At 22 I didn't rate above a gentleman's C on any of them.

I was probably no worse than millions of my contemporaries in this regard, privilege-laden as we were. Maybe I was even above average for all Americans taken together. The comparison counts for little, however. Our grades for living well, living responsibly, are not assigned on a curve. They are measured against a gold standard. Truth be known, the Johnnie A of those days was a bit spoiled, when you looked behind the polite and prayerful exterior. Tough lessons awaited me—as they did my generation and our country.

CHAPTER 6

ANSWERING THE CALL

Psalms 146:3

Graduating from Principia College in June 1966, I did my final summer as a camp counselor in Colorado, back to Backbone one last time; got engaged to Donna D'Evelyn of Bakersfield, California, my college sweetheart; and entered Naval Officer Candidate School that November. Donna and I were married on a weekend leave the following spring, hurrying between my OCS graduation and my start date for submarine training. By Thanksgiving Day 1967 I was aboard the USS *Bonefish*, SS-582, a diesel-powered attack submarine headed for Japan by way of the Vietnam war zone.

My skippers on *Bonefish*, Bob Gavazzi and Jim Blanchard, taught me a lot about responsibility without ever using the word. I believed strongly (then and now) in our country's military commitment in Southeast Asia as a blocking move against the global communist threat posed by the Soviet Union. I was proud to be able to do my part. Duty at sea brought hourly lessons in Reality 101.

THREE GENERATIONS OF McCAINS

U.S. submarine forces in those years played mainly a nuclear-deterrent and intelligence-gathering role. In my ship's case, that meant tracking Red Chinese naval activity in the Yellow Sea. When North Korea seized the *USS Pueblo* in January 1968, we were the closest American military unit. For some hours a shooting war seemed imminent.

Returning to home port in Hawaii, I continued learning by trial and error about how to be a good husband, and was soon an expectant father. Our daughter Tina was born at Pearl Harbor in February1969. Much of my off-duty time was spent in Bible study and writing about spiritual topics, monitoring tensions between my dad's youth camps and unsupportive church authorities, and following mainland political news—which was harder to do in mid-Pacific back then, without satellite television or the Internet.

"What I did in the war" was not remotely comparable with the sacrifices of men I'd known at college. Among them were John Sweet, killed in action; Peter Gans, severely wounded and hospitalized for long months of recovery; and Allen Orcutt, exhausted from flying countless helicopter missions near the DMZ, and whose wife ran off with another man while Allen was in Vietnam.

On the sub base one day, I attended a conference where the main speaker was the US Pacific commander, Admiral John S. McCain, Jr. The father of this famed submariner had been an admiral before him, and we all knew about his son, the Navy pilot being held prisoner in Hanoi. The toll this war must be taking on them was unimaginable to me. My family's three-generation naval tradition was nothing to theirs. Taking my uniform off, when the time came, would be okay. Ashore and a civilian: that's what I was cut out for.

Until then my only contribution of note—other than standing a lot of night watches at sea with my father's stern voice always echoing: "On a submarine every man has the other 80 men's lives in his hands, no margin for error"—would be made with a typewriter.

TYPEWRITER COMBAT

General Electric was devoting an issue of its national public-affairs quarterly, *GE Forum*, to opposing views about student radicals and the anti-war movement. Carl Oglesby, the former president of Students for a Democratic Society and a member of the International War Crimes Tribunal, was to give one side. An editor at GE who knew our family invited me to present the other.

Oglesby's article argued that the "rebellion of American youth" represented a "concerned and informed people… coming explosively into existence." For them, he concluded, "revolution is where it's at."

My piece made the case for "moral activism… working inside the system from the positive standpoint that America is not corrupt, but only unfulfilled." Callow but earnest, I called myself "an American revolutionary of the New Right," devoted to "the eternal work of exalting the spirit of man."

Donna Andrews covered home

While it was hardly the cover of *Time*, that article ended up making a huge difference in my life. As my active-duty hitch came to an end in the final weeks of 1969, Donna and I found ourselves back in Missouri, where I was about to give newspapering a try on the *Kansas City Star*. Out of the blue, White House press secretary Ron Ziegler phoned me with an invitation to come and interview for a job. It turned out that John Ehrlichman, the President's domestic policy chief and a patron of the Andrews camps, had recommended me on the strength of my *GE Forum* piece. So began my Nixon odyssey.

In Washington over the next four years, Donna and I would bring daughter Jennifer and son Daniel into the world; buy a home in suburban Bethesda after outgrowing two rentals; and learn of the health problems that were soon to take from us both my mother and her father in their fifties—all the while, constantly pinching ourselves at the historic events and personalities that were part of our daily lives.

After a stormy twelve months as Ziegler's personal aide, worried that he might fire me any day, I "failed upward" into the speechwriting operation in early 1971. As campus unrest seethed and the 18-year-old vote was due to come online for election year 1972, Nixon's chief speechwriter Raymond Price wanted to add an under-30 utility man. I and other young staffers were asked to recommend applicants. When none of those panned out, Price and Ziegler settled on me. It was essentially an affirmative-action hire—but I wasn't too proud to say yes.

My first effort as a presidential ghost, a patriotic talk to the Daughters of the American Revolution, gets barely a D in the grade book of painful memory. Sitting there in agony as President Nixon stumbled through my clumsy sentences—majestic to the eye but in no way written for the ear—renewed my fears of getting ignominiously canned. But Price was a patient editor and coach, senior colleagues William Safire and Patrick Buchanan were generous with me, and gradually I learned the craft.

Henry Kissinger for some reason took a liking to me. "Andrews is a natural at the flag-waving stuff," he jabbed—not exactly a compliment—and in time I became the designated hitter for Nixon's periodic televised reports to the nation about America's fighting withdrawal from Vietnam. This in turn led to a coveted seat on Air Force One for the Moscow summit meeting with Leonid Brezhnev in May 1972.

We flew into the Soviet Union via Iran and out via Poland, two countries that were then quiet but which would become flashpoints later in the decade. Safire was along to write the speeches needed en route. I was to draft RN's address to a joint session of Congress for the evening of June 1, immediately after we landed in Washington from Warsaw.

Moscow was surreal. Cold warrior and anti-communist that I was, shaped by such episodes of Soviet brutality as the Hungarian uprising of 1956, the Cuban missile crisis of 1962, and the Prague Spring of 1968, the place repulsed me. The Russian people we met, on the other hand, were easy to like. Yet nothing but diplomatic courtesy made me raise a glass when US-Soviet friendship was toasted.

Later I would come to regard Richard Nixon's soft policy of détente with the Soviets, including an ABM treaty that locked in their advantage on missile defense, as more to his discredit than the law-breaking that finally toppled him. At the time, though, our delegation was buoyed with enthusiasm at bringing home agreements for the "full generation of peace" that was to be the President's reelection theme in the coming campaign. Aboard the presidential jet as we flew the Atlantic inbound to Washington, I was called to his cabin to make final changes on the speech.

SEEDS OF DISASTER

News footage of Nixon landing by helicopter at the Capitol that night, and receiving an ovation inside before starting to speak, constitutes the opening scene of *All the President's Men,* the film version of Bob Woodward and Carl Bernstein's book about RN's downfall. The movie then cuts to a reenactment of the burglars from CREEP, his campaign committee, even then inside Democratic headquarters at the Watergate office building, planting illegal wiretaps.

Could we but know it, with tragic irony worthy of Shakespeare, the seeds of disaster were being sown at the very moment of triumph. But the rest of 1972 was a heady chapter in my life. After helping write the president's acceptance speech at the Republican National Convention in Miami, I traveled extensively with him on the campaign trail as RN cruised to victory over Democratic challenger George McGovern.

Yet there was an ominous shadow over all of it for me from the slowly building Watergate scandal. From the first announcement of the burglars' arrest in mid-June, something made me take the matter more seriously than most others on the staff seemed to. The storm broke over all of us with full force in the early weeks of 1973. By late summer, when I was drafting that "contrition" speech which the President never gave, a sense of doom was becoming harder to avoid inside Fort Nixon.

"At least there's Vice President Agnew if RN doesn't survive," some of us told each other. Then bribery charges pulled him down. I had the distasteful assignment (a morale-breaker as far as my own continuation on the job was concerned) of writing the resignation speech that Spiro T. Agnew delivered to a national television audience on October 10. The guidelines Nixon personally provided me for how that nasty business should be spun proved prophetic, ten months later, of the explanation he would give the American people for his own resignation.

Whom would he nominate to fill the vacancy? Speechwriters were told to work up materials on Gov. Nelson Rockefeller of New York, Gov. Ronald Reagan of California, former Texas governor and now Treasury Secretary John Connally, and House Minority Leader Gerald Ford. It was Ford, judged most easily confirmable by congressional Democrats, who got the call. That was the last thing I worked on at the White House. I had had it. My final day on the staff was the day the new vice president took office, December 7, 1973.

CHAPTER 7

BATTLEFIELD OF IDEAS

II Corinthians 10:4,5

Exiting a presidential staff, one doesn't lack for job possibilities. Options for this disillusioned 29-year-old scribbler in early 1974 included something with William F. Buckley at *National Review* in New York; an opening on the Washington staff of his brother, Sen. James Buckley; and a position with Secretary of State Henry Kissinger.

Flattering as these were, I wanted out. I had had it with all things Potomac or East Coast. I yearned to go back to Backbone. When my father urged me to come to work for him in Denver, it felt right. In March 1974 I became communications director for Adventure Unlimited, the youth ministry that had grown from my dad's camp ventures.

The next few years found me unplugged politically, for the most part, yet experiencing a rich time of personal growth and preparation for challenges to come. Helping direct the mountain camps and local teen chapters forced me to learn management, afforded plenty of time in the high country, and led to a more searching encounter with our family's Christian Science religion, which I began to question.

Along with teaching Sunday school, I supported our kids in sports and Scouts; wrote occasionally for *National Review* and the Denver papers; and read voraciously on American history and biography, constitutional principles, conservative ideas, and Christian thought. The first part of my thirties became a self-paced seminar putting intellectual and spiritual structure around the lived experiences of my twenties. It was like catching up with the textbook, *after* having done the lab.

Through friendships formed over breakfast at the Arapahoe County Republican Men's Club, I was soon volunteering on campaigns for county commissioner, governor, and Congress.[30] But I was merely a pro-Reagan spectator when the Californian sought to wrest the GOP nomination from President Ford in 1976. In the early stages of 1980 (confessing it now with chagrin), I wasn't with the Gipper at all, but was listed as an on-call writer for his chief rival and eventual running mate, George H. W. Bush, who had befriended me in Watergate days. It was former speechwriting colleague David Gergen who recruited me to the Bush team. In the end I was glad they never utilized me.

Ronald Reagan's accession to the White House in January 1981 coincided with the end of the line for me at Adventure Unlimited. My political itch had combined with a crisis of faith and troubles in our marriage to make a career change seem urgent. I was the trapped feel-

ing of an eaglet desperate to hatch. But quitting my father's employ was tough. "Cap," as everyone called the one-time submariner, was a visionary idealist, a compelling leader, and the strongest-willed man I've ever known. It hurt him to have his son walk away, yet he received my decision with gentleness and grace.

John Andrews Sr. at camp

I guess Dad sensed, without knowing all the details, that Johnnie A had come to the point of hatch or rot.[31] Out of the egg, out of the nest, and into uncertain flight I went, with his blessing.

THINK TANKS

Imprimis, the monthly speech digest of Hillsdale College, had long been high on my reading list. A visit to Hillsdale's Michigan campus led to a job offer from George C. Roche III, the Coloradan who had built the little school into a beacon for liberty since becoming its president in 1971. I became editor of *Imprimis*, director of campus seminars, and Roche's point man to help create the Shavano Institute at Keystone, Colorado, envisioned as a sort of Aspen Institute of the right.

Those years of commuting between Denver and Detroit were priceless to me as an impromptu grad degree in both free-market ideas and nonprofit entreneurship. George Roche, who died brokenhearted in 2005 amidst unproven allegations of scandal, has my enduring gratitude. Flawed as the man may have been, his lifework contributed to the renewal of responsibility in America.

Out of the Hillsdale and Shavano crucible came my opportunity to start one of the first state-based conservative think tanks, the Independence Institute, in 1985. By then the union of "free and independent states" proclaimed by the Declaration of Independence was in better condition than it had been in the Vietnam and Watergate aftermath a decade earlier. But there was still a need for fresh, principled thinking in state capitals, and a few of us in Colorado set out to meet it.

Partnering with my wife's brother, David D'Evelyn, and aided by an early grant from Donald Rumsfeld, I mobilized intellectual minutemen—among them an Austrian-school economist from the University of Colorado and a policy analyst from Coors Brewing—to begin offering policy alternatives to liberalism in state government. Similar institutes were being established at about the same time in Illinois, South Carolina, and Washington State. Before long, startup aspirants from would-be think tanks in Indiana, Texas, and Nevada were coming to us for guidance. The Heritage Foundation took notice. Independence was launched!

Now in its 26th year, ably led in latter days by Tom Tancredo and currently by Jon Caldara, the Independence Institute is acknowledged as the premier conservative voice on Colorado issues. Through its influence, Coloradans today lean less to collective or coercive policy approaches and more toward decentralized, voluntary solutions than they otherwise would. The institute is an example of the American initiative and innovation cited 175 years ago by Alexis de Tocqueville as one of the springs of our country's vitality. I will always have fatherly feelings for it.

ROOKIE CANDIDATE

Independence Institute became a founding member of State Policy Network, an alliance that now encompasses free-market think tanks in all 50 states. I took an early turn as alliance chairman. From national contacts of that kind, from study trips to the Soviet Union and South Korea and a Nicaragua policy handbook we published, from my constant immersion in Colorado's issue debate, and from my appointment by President Reagan to the Intergovernmental Advisory Council on Education, the idea of a political race began to grow on me.

It was the spring of 1990. The timing was hasty, funding was problematic, and the casting seemed unlikely for a guy with my ivory-tower air and sharp-edged conservative reputation. Someone would have to run the institute while I ran a campaign. Donna had deep reservations. I plunged anyway, announcing my candidacy on April 19, 1990, for the Republican nomination for Governor of Colorado at the state convention in June.

Gov. Roy Romer, the Democrat incumbent, was riding high in the polls after a strong first term. Most of the likely Republican challengers had taken a pass. Colorado Springs mayor Bob Isaac, a tax-hiking moderate, was being courted by GOP state chairman Bruce Benson to take on Romer, but when I got into the race, Isaac decided not to. Why not see if Andrews and his Freedom Agenda could pull an upset?

After seven hectic weeks of rallying party audiences across the state with my "Hunt for Romer November" stump speech, wearing an old submarine jacket, I won the nomination on June 9 with 65 percent of the delegate vote. Former congressman Mike Strang took 28 percent, two points shy of what he needed to force us to a primary in August. Strang came up short because of libertarian gadfly and stuntman Robin Heid, who got the other 7% after sky-diving into the convention parking lot.

If we had been climbing a Fourteener, that was timberline. The rugged ridge leading to election night, 150 days away, would test whether this unknown political rookie could woo a majority of voters away from the wily and popular incumbent. I could not. My steep learning curve, our mistakes, his breaks, Iraq's invasion of Kuwait, President Bush's broken promise on taxes, a rebounding Colorado economy, and the 5:1 funding advantage Democrats enjoyed, added up to a landslide of 60-plus percent for Gov. Romer when it was all over.

Losing hurts like the dickens, even when you think you're prepared for it. I was not myself for a while. Remember the beard Al Gore grew after losing to Bush in 2000? Photographs exist of me, bearded as if trying to hide from the world, in late 1990. Republicans above and below me on the ticket, Hank Brown for Senate and Gale Norton for attorney general, had won while Andrews for governor was getting trounced. The Independence Institute needed reviving, and I had overtaxed some family relationships. It was a costly year in a number of ways, and a humbling one.

FAILING TO SUMMIT

Few peaks, physical or figurative, have ever turned me back— but Mount Governor did. Yet the failure to summit is never a flat failure; from the altitude gained, you start the next ascent. There was satisfaction in seeing two constitutional reforms I had championed get far more votes than I did. Coloradans adopted a term- limits amendment by a wide margin, and they nearly passed the Taxpayer's Bill of Rights, a limitation on spending and taxes that did prevail two years later.

"Andrews' ideas may win even if he doesn't," veteran political writer Peter Blake had predicted in the *Rocky Mountain News* late in the race. So it proved, not only on those two ballot measures but also on several of my other campaign issues, from school choice to worker's compensation, which moved our way in coming years.

Formidable as an opponent, Roy Romer was gracious to me in triumph. "You will have other opportunities," he said consolingly on election night, recalling that his victory for governor in 1986 had come 20 years after a lopsided defeat for US Senate. I was touched by the Democrat's gesture but dubious that anything similar awaited this dejected Republican. The political bus wouldn't be stopping for me again as best I could foresee, but that was fine. My goal had always been seeing the American promise more fully realized, not holding public office for its own sake.

As the Clinton-Gingrich years came on, new chances for advancing that goal opened up to me. I was invited to San Antonio for a year when the Texas Public Policy Foundation, a startup I had mentored in the '80s, needed an interim chief executive. Home again in Denver, I convinced cable television pioneer Bob Magness of Tele-Communications Inc. (TCI) to experiment with conservative-leaning public affairs programming for his 18 million subscribers across the country.

TCI News was born, and my first hire was producer Bob Chitester, the man behind Milton Friedman's legendary *Free to Choose* television series and book. Our two-year national run with *Damn Right*, David Asman's nightly magazine show from an imaginary diner, and *Race for the Presidency*, hosted weekly by Clifford May, was an early indication of the audience potential that was soon to be realized in spectacular fashion by Rupert Murdock and Roger Ailes with the Fox News Channel. Asman and a number of other TCI News alumni are with Fox today. For bipartisan balance in our presidential series, I brought on leading Democrats such as Richard Lamm and Gary Hart as cohosts.

The venture ended with Magness's untimely death in 1997, just as Fox News was taking off. I had never worked in front of the camera at TCI. My consolation prize was the opportunity to create for Colorado Public Television the daily *Head On* mini-debates, where I traded quick shots on current issues with lefty pundit Dani Newsum. The program still airs statewide, these days with Susan Barnes-Gelt as my friendly adversary.

CHAPTER 8

VOTED IN

Isaiah 33:22

olorado Republicans, shut out of the governor's office since 1974, sensed that 1998 might be their moment. Gov. Roy Romer, who had won a third term against Bruce Benson in 1994, was barred from running again by the constitutional term limit I had helped enact. State Treasurer Bill Owens looked to be the likely GOP nominee against Lt. Gov. Gail Schoettler. Our party was on a roll nationally. Now we might finally recapture executive power in Denver.

Ever since his days as a young state representative a dozen years before, Owens had been close to the Independence Institute and an ally of mine. He came out for the Taxpayer's Bill of Rights when many Republicans wouldn't. Bill was a skillful politician, principled yet personable. I wrote an article speculating that if elected, he could be our state's version of a change-implementing Reagan who would build on my earlier efforts vision-casting Goldwater. But holding elected office myself, as a result of the dominoes soon to fall, never crossed my mind.

SENATE DISTRICT 27

At a Texas expatriates lawn party—who knows why?—I ran into state Sen. Mike Coffman, who represented our part of the south suburbs. Coffman said he'd be running for Treasurer as Bill Owens' term ended that year, and suggested I seek appointment to the Senate vacancy in the event he won. I thought little more about the idea during an eventful summer that included my father's sudden passing at 78, our son's wedding, the failing health of Donna's mother, and an upheaval in our family finances.

It wasn't until a week before the election, with Owens and Coffman both polling well, that we saw our way clear for my bid in Senate District 27. Note the word "we." I had learned a lot about marital part-

*Colorado State Sen.
John Andrews*

nership—and about Christian introspection and prayer since my impulsive gubernatorial run in 1990. The old Johnnie A ambition wasn't gone. But an attitude of "Thy will not mine" made this candidacy different.

The results happily differed too. I topped a field of six in the December 3 vacancy convention. On December 30 I was sworn into the Colorado General Assembly. In brief remarks after the ceremony, I quoted Sir Thomas More (as portrayed in Robert Bolt's play, *A Man for All Seasons*) about what such an act of solemn swearing means: "When a man takes an oath, he's holding his own self in his own hands. Like water."[32] My implicit reference to the impeachment for perjury (false swearing) then facing President Bill Clinton was noted by John Sanko in the next day's *Rocky Mountain News*.

Responsibility and freedom, indivisible and indispensable, had gained a new soldier on the Colorado political battlefield. When Governor-elect Owens took over the capitol's first floor as our state's Gipper, I'd be upstairs on the legislative floor as his Goldwater. Backbone had its senator.

UNDER THE GOLD DOME

As Ray Powers, a conservative from Colorado Springs, assumed the Senate President's gavel from Greeley moderate Tom Norton in January 1999, our Republican caucus held a comfortable 20-15 majority. We also enjoyed the novel distinction of standing to the right of the

House Republicans, who had just picked the centrist Russell George of Rifle as their speaker. For years the Senate had been *less* Reaganite than the House.

My committee assignments from Powers and Majority Leader Tom Blickensderfer fit the moment well. With the new governor pushing a school accountability plan and a series of tax cuts, I would sit on both Education and Finance. Judiciary, chaired by matronly liberal Dottie Wham of Denver (with whom I agreed on virtually nothing), would become my venue for proposing the nation's first term limit on judges. In that committee I made friends with Ed Perlmutter, a Democrat from Golden who is now in Congress.

I was close to future Republican congressmen Marilyn Musgrave and Doug Lamborn as well. My office mate and best legislative ally was fellow freshman Mark Hillman, a young bachelor wheat farmer from Burlington. Mark had sought me out at the Independence Institute earlier in the decade, when I was a gubernatorial also ran and he was an aspiring political writer. Our bond was a shared interest in translating conservative ideas into workable policy.

That is not an easy translation to make, as I quickly found. For some of us like Musgrave, Lamborn, Hillman, and me, ideas such as responsibility and freedom, limited government and economic liberty are stars to steer by. For too many in our party, though, these things tended to be little more than twinkles in the sky, easily ignored when "facts on the ground" dictate a less principled course.

Incumbency for its own sake, the height of irresponsibility, was already beginning to seduce the Republican Congress in those years. GOP legislators in Colorado stood much steadier, thanks in part to constitutional restraints on taxes and spending and to the damping of careerist incentives by term limits.

Early in Bill Owens' term there was also a pent-up agenda for rightward reform that kept our side focused and unified. We rebated billions of dollars to taxpayers, expanded charter schools, toughened education standards, and passed a long-overdue highway program.

Owens' office wasn't pleased when Perlmutter and I won a court ruling that put the governor's road bonds to a popular vote, but the measure was easily approved (with my support) and became a stepping-stone to Bill's reelection.

My proudest success that first year was toll lanes with variable rates for peak and off-peak hours, a market solution for congestion on Denver's north metro freeways. "HOT lanes," as they were called, heated up the debate over incentive-based approaches for transportation and mobility, but they left the bureaucracy cold. Although my 1999 bill called for implementation in 18 months, the lanes didn't open until 2006, after I had left office and fully seven years from enactment.

LESSONS OF LEADERSHIP

Politics runs on a strange clock, glacial at one moment and warp-speed the next. By June 2000, Owens' popularity was already faltering among Republicans after his support of a gun-control bill following the Columbine massacre. By November 2000, the Colorado political situation had become advantage: Democrats. They captured the state Senate for the first time in 40 years and won their Amendment 23 ballot issue to escalate education spending, a danger to budget discipline under our Taxpayer's Bill of Rights (TABOR).

I awoke the morning after election day with mixed emotions. I felt honored to have won my own four-year Senate term, and pleased to have the votes in hand to be elected Republican leader. But I was sobered to realize it was now the minority, not the majority, that I would lead. With Mark Hillman as my No. 2, we played the loyal opposition against President Stan Matsunaka and his Democrats for the next two sessions. I gave each GOP senator a red, white, and blue calendar cube—tear-off notepads counting down the days until we could take back control in November 2002. When the day came, our party achieved the goal with nothing to spare, returning to the majority 18-17 as Gov. Owens won his second term in a landslide.

"Republicans Rule," proclaimed the headlines. US Sen. Wayne Allard, considered an underdog, was reelected, and the new congressional seat Colorado had gained in redistricting went our way as Bob Beauprez won by a whisker. Yet there was quiet concern over some state Senate races that got away from us, and over the erosion of our state House majority for the fourth straight election cycle. Democrats also won another strategically important ballot issue, Amendment 27, which tilted the state's campaign finance law sharply in favor of labor unions and against business.

Structural reforms of that kind—whether drawn wisely or, as in this case, to my judgment, unwisely—make a far greater difference than the ordinary law or program. They can change the whole landscape of self-government. They absorbed me throughout my time as a senator.

Believing as I do that personal responsibility is the cornerstone of a free society and the essence of living well, I had little interest in exploring what government can do *for* people. What it can do *to* them, unless constantly restrained, concerned me far more.

My goal was to see political power more effectively deployed in protecting the open space of ordered liberty where individuals can choose responsibly and act for themselves. When colleagues chose me as Senate President for 2003-2004, I wanted this to be the Andrews signature.

Signing with a flourish is problematic when you have co-signers, however. Senate Republican Majority Leader Norma Anderson, an imperious moderate from Lakewood who delighted in her nickname of "Dragon Lady," lost no love for me. GOP House Speaker Lola Spradley, a southern Colorado businesswoman and the first female to lead the Colorado House of Representatives, was always a trustworthy partner but not inclined to think as a visionary conservative. We found Gov. Bill Owens less aggressive on state issues than in his first term, preoccupied initially with presidential hopes and later with a painful marital breakup. The two Democratic minority leaders, Sen.

Joan Fitz-Gerald of Genessee and Rep. Andrew Romanoff of Denver, were implacable adversaries to all of us.

In our constitutional republic, lawmakers can't simply order people to be more responsible and less dependent, to balance rights with duties, to act self-reliant instead of entitled. But there is still an important character-shaping function to everything government does and doesn't do. Statecraft is still soulcraft, as George Will has said.[33] Public policy provides important signals and incentives. During the two 120-day sessions that I'd be presiding—with term limits set to retire me after 2004[34]—I prioritized more than a dozen goals, 14 to be exact.

This was an ambitious agenda well beyond what we could realistically achieve. But by aiming high we hoped to surprise our doubters, and we did so. Going in, I wanted to see our state:

- Adopt education vouchers
- Expand patient choice in health care
- Strengthen property rights
- Discourage illegal immigration
- Curb union power

and

- Extend concealed-carry permits for handguns
- Require parental notification for minors seeking an abortion
- Preserve the constitutional restraints on taxes and spending
- Enact a redistricting bill to improve congressional representation

and

- Improve school boards and the transit district by partisan elections
- Strengthen the safeguards against lobbying abuses and voter fraud
- Enact court reform including judicial term limits
- Initiate market reforms for Medicaid

- Establish color-blind state hiring, contracting, and college admissions to end racial preferences.

Our score was a respectable 9 out of 14. Only on the last five goals was nothing achieved during my tenure as President. The batting average drops off, however, when you remember that our two biggest achievements, education vouchers and redistricting, were annulled by politicized justices on the Colorado Supreme Court, who acceded to what we felt were spurious legal arguments by Democrats.

Our success in resisting a strike at the Taxpayer's Bill of Rights and a raid on the state treasury was also short-lived. That very result ensued a few months after I left the Senate in 2005, when a bipartisan spenders coalition persuaded voters to waive TABOR's revenue limits until 2011 and permanently weaken its fiscal restraints.

CHAPTER 9

THE SLOW LEARNER

Ecclesiastes 12:14

"All back full!" On a ship at sea, after the command is given to reverse the engines, your forward progress doesn't stop instantly. But up on the bridge you can feel "the way come off her" as the screws bite and the water's motion along the hull decreases. You sense the change of direction before you see it. That's how 2004 was for Republicans in Colorado and, to some extent, across the country.

My final year as Senate President was taken up with defensive actions in the spring against the spending lobby and in the fall against an all-out Democratic drive to take the legislature. President George W. Bush appeared to be in trouble for reelection after governing less conservatively than most had expected. He eked out a win, but in our state the election was GOP disaster top to bottom. Democrats retook the state Senate by one vote and won the House for the first time since 1974, as well as switching a congressional seat and a U.S. Senator in their favor. Accompanying the bad numbers was an ominous feeling that things could get worse before they got better, so nearly dead in the water did the conservative movement seem.

The title of private citizen, as honorable a station as any American can occupy, was mine again on January 12, 2005, when school voucher champion Nancy Spence succeeded me in the Senate and jubilant Democrats elevated Irish brawler Joan Fitz-Gerald to the President's chair. I was glad for Donna's sake that the intensity of our life the past six years could now ease up a bit, especially since the care of her ailing mother had become so demanding. I also looked forward to more time with little Ian Michael, Daniel and Stephanie's son, who had recently turned two. Out of that political transition and those family thoughts came the impetus for this book on responsibility.

CHARACTER COUNTS

Why had the conservative movement's "way come off"? Some would say the right had worked itself out of a job, after largely prevailing against the communist evil empire abroad and the unlimited growth of government at home. Americans, by this logic, were simply moving on with a new shopping list to a different aisle in the political supermarket.

Others would say the conservative brand was discredited after years of a congressional spending spree, corruption charges, and messy foreign entanglements. Straighten up, get back to walking our talk, and we'd soon regain headway, according to this diagnosis.

Both explanations made sense up to a point. But in thinking about the problem, thinking harder than I'd ever done before, I felt there was something more. I was hosting Backbone Radio every week, writing for the *Denver Post* every other Sunday, doing daily TV commentaries, and learning to blog. Relief from operational duties was giving me time for deep reflection such as I hadn't had in decades.

I had also become a fellow of the Claremont Institute for the Study of Statesmanship and Political Philosophy, helping carry their insights about the American founding to state capitals and Congress. Our Founders, it seemed to me, wouldn't recognize the morally flaccid country we've become. Tocqueville wouldn't. Lincoln wouldn't. Where was the alarm on the right about that?

What government should or shouldn't do is an important question for keeping America true to itself. But too narrow a focus on that question has tended to distract conservatives from one that's even more important: *What qualities of character are essential to sustain a free and good society?*

Families and other mediating institutions, civic virtue, spiritual rigor, and the overall moral tone of our common life—citizens must hold these priorities as dear as political action, if we're not to go the way of Glubb's and Tytler's warnings. During the past three decades, the responsible remnant sensed this and stirred to action across a broad front, irrespective of organizational charts and ideological labels. Increasingly, in the years since I left public office, building the remnant's effectiveness and cohesion has taken on greater urgency for me than party work.

Would Tocqueville recognize us?

MY REPORT CARD

To have devoted my life to protecting, studying, celebrating, and serving America, a country built on personal responsibility like no other before it, and to have reached age 60, a grandfather with a gilded resume, before finally recognizing America's treasure—that's what makes me call myself a slow learner.

"For me, it's no longer freedom that is the master value. It is freedom's obverse, responsibility." I am grateful to have come to the point where I could make that emphatic declaration in an earlier chapter. But I am chagrined to think how long it took me to get there. The paradox of success no doubt contributed to my persistent complacency about something that was, in retrospect, so obvious and so indispensable all along.

And it seems to me that America's largely charmed life during our first two centuries must have had exactly the same effect on us as a people. When you're gliding aloft, seemingly without effort, it's easy to forget the principle of the airfoil that makes the wings work. The paradox of success strikes again.

So now for the report card: What overall grade do I give myself on assuming the fullness of responsibility over the course of the life that I've sketched in these pages, the marking period 1944-2011? *I can't honestly go higher than a B-. Maybe only a C+.*

Too harsh? I don't think so. As stated at the outset, this is graded to an objective high standard, not on a comparative curve. Nor is the mark skewed by hindsight. It's measured against what was realistically responsible at the time, with the inner resources I know I had and the information I know I possessed. It's a wakeup call for the learner, tough love for the person in the mirror. Care to try it?

The higher we score on the scale of character, the more fit we are for freedom—and the less need there is for intrusive restrictions by government. Or by employers, clergy, spouses or parents, teachers or wardens. This is what John Adams meant when he said, in effect, that our easy-riding constitution would only work for a people who ride themselves hard.[35] Or to put it another way, life is a bank: Only what you deposit in responsibility can you withdraw in trust. Overdraw too often and your account's closed.

Among my criteria for fully responsible conduct in the areas of our lives and the situations we face, remember, were things like considering others and knowing it's not all about us; having the awareness and fortitude to self-criticize and self-correct; keeping hold of reality and free of self-deception. Considered this way, some of life's "exams" are easy to grade, if painful to face. Other big tests elude a clear mark, yielding a murky "incomplete."

For example, when I broke my marriage vows, betraying my wife and hurting our children, the grade was an ugly F. The "account closed" that I deserved was mercifully stayed. On the other hand, the grade was something close to an A, I'd like to think, when I volunteered for military service in wartime and said made the case in print for all those in my generation who did likewise.

But how genuinely responsible was my public protest resignation from Nixon's staff during Watergate? How well did I meet the responsibility ethic with my generalship in such bitter legislative battles as the 2003 redistricting bill and the 2004 budget crisis? Those tests weigh in a subtler balance.

NOT JUST SHOWING UP

Maybe it's true, as Woody Allen said, that 80 percent of life is just showing up. But are you satisfied to be an 80-percenter? Me neither. That final 20 percent is where we excel or not. That's where we make the difference for those who depend on us.

"Just showing up" scarcely qualifies for the greatness of nations, either. The question for America in this new century isn't whether we'll still be on the map; we will. The question is whether we will continue to lead, whether we will remain a beacon for mankind's aspirations.

Responsibility involves measuring up as well as showing up. It starts with being there, certainly. But it also means being our best and doing our best. Not necessarily *the* best, but at least *our* best. Everyone can't finish first, but no one is excused from finishing if humanly possible. Nor is merely doing as well as the next guy, good enough. Individual potential is the yardstick. From those who are given more, more is expected.

I could show you the exact spot where we were standing in the activity room at my high school, on the day when our faculty adviser quizzed the student council—led by me, their proud president—about preparations for next week's big winter dance. What's being done about this, this, and this, John? You mean the decorations aren't ordered yet and the invitations aren't out yet? And the dance is when?

I wanted to sink through the floor. The event would obviously have to be cancelled. It turned out there was more to being student body president than just showing up for meetings. The academic ace had flunked real-life responsibility that day. The track star had dropped the baton bigtime. As a learning experience, though, this was a life-changer, and not very costly. I was never the same person again—and when it came time for the spring carnival, we didn't blow it.

Responsibility and irresponsibility seldom come flagged with colored lights as we face life's choices. The very moment of choice is often imperceptible. This is true for us as individuals, and still more so in our collective decisions or habits. For America as a country, the complexity is worse yet. The point of this chapter and the next one is to challenge us to see that and consciously correct for it.

In itself, an Andrews ethical autopsy for its own sake holds little interest for readers. What I hope to do in this report-card exercise is to illustrate the need for introspection as we mobilize Element R. True responsibility is unfortunately not instinctive. We must demand it of ourselves and of each other. Living responsibly requires constant, purposeful application.

OUTCOMES, NOT INTENTIONS

In the family, up to age 22 when I became a naval officer and a married man, I'm afraid that as a son and brother I rated only a C, a passing grade for having done what was required but not much more. Friendly with my brother but not insightful about him as a person, politely distant from both my sisters, and no more than superficially affectionate to our mother, I typified the gifted, privileged, self-absorbed young guy.

For the summer of 1965, ahead of my senior year in college, I earnestly wanted to be a civil-rights volunteer in Mississippi. My father insisted on me working for him at camp in Colorado instead, and I went along. How to grade that one? Perhaps an A for filial obedience—but a D for citizenship. Reaching higher and grasping opportunities, not just meeting our obvious obligations, ideally defines responsibility. The memory of that road not taken leaves me uneasy.

So does my slow-learner courtship of Donna at that same period. Responsibility understood as realistic maturity, eyes wide open to the rightness and fitness of things, would have had me asking Mr. and Mrs. D'Evelyn for their daughter's hand a year sooner than I did. I chose well, by the grace of God, but indecisively. Give it a B. Looking back, I see a moral tentativeness at work in me in several ways, a doubleness that would later prove costly.

Knowing our own motives at a crisis or a crossroads is very difficult. Rationalization is powerful. Few but saints have reliable self-knowledge under pressure. Why did I quit Nixon's staff and turn on him? Why did I leave the church our family had served for a century? Why wasn't I a better husband and father? Why did I run for governor? Why did I gamble for high stakes at critical moments in the Senate? How far short of a top grade, A for responsible American, did I come on each of those tests?

The grade isn't given merely or even mainly for motives, of course. That's one of the worst fallacies of liberalism—the confusion of intentions with results. Responsible action is evaluated first by objective outcomes. The subjectivity of what you *meant* to do, whether achieved or not, is not negligible—but it's secondary.

History for each of us and for all of us together is the product of countless human choices in the gray area where purpose, performance, potentiality, and providence converge. That grayness obscures moral certainty. Yet the effort for self-understanding is never in vain. It yields growth and counteracts entropy. It is an effort we cannot responsibly avoid as persons or as a people.

NO PARAGON

Take my departure from the White House staff in late 1973. The abdication of personal responsibility by President Nixon and his men was inexorably ruining him and bringing the country toward its irresponsible nadir. I was the conscience-stricken young speechwriter who resigned soon after the Saturday Night Massacre and the disgrace of Vice President Agnew. I then went public with tough criticisms of the moral vacuum at the top, including a call for Nixon's resignation or impeachment. But does that make me a paragon of responsibility? Not necessarily.

As early as July 1972, just weeks after the Watergate burglars were arrested, I got a tip that culpability might reach into the White House staff. Staff attorney Egil Krogh, a mentor of mine and himself culpable as head of the "plumbers unit" illegally chasing national security leaks, nervously advised me to take the matter to White House counsel John Dean.[36] Dean, who would later turn state's evidence as mastermind of the coverup, told me not to worry. The rumor was baseless and I should forget it, he said. So I tried to. How responsible was that?

Fast forward to April 1973. The scandal had metastasized, Dean had been fired, and Nixon's entire presidency was now endangered. Worse was to come, according to gossip in the speechwriting shop, some of it fed by the back-channel friendship of David Gergen, No. 2 on our staff, with *Washington Post* investigative reporter Bob Woodward. At an evening reception, catching a moment to speak personally with the President, I stammered out my fears. It was like trying to talk with one of the portraits on the East Room wall—nothing. Back to work I went the next day, loyally "supporting the presidential office" and swallowing my misgivings about the man. How responsible was that?

Perhaps in fact it was the most responsible thing a very junior, very inexperienced, very naïve underling in the service of the chief executive of the United States of America could have done right then. Perhaps shutting up and staying with the ship and working alongside all those other heartsick staffers to keep her afloat until the very moment the skipper left the bridge, the day of Nixon's resignation on August 8, 1974—and not quitting as I did the previous December—would really have been a truer course of responsibility than the one I took.

I think I know the answer. I think that's *not* so. But to this day I can't claim to be certain. What if my own showy resignation was really more about John the Righteous than about the rule of law and fidelity to the Constitution? Opinion page of the *Washington Post*, front page of the *New York Times*, CBS Morning News and PBS on Friday night, Tom

Brokaw calling me at home and the "My Turn" column in *Newsweek*—it was all quite flattering to this self-styled "American revolutionary of the New Right" who had been toiling in anonymity at 1600 Pennsylvania Avenue and second-guessing himself for a decade about that summer in Mississippi that never was.

What if my December exit from the writing staff was really prompted less by moral outrage than by burnout and boyish disillusionment? What if my January and February weeks in the media limelight were not so much a brave indictment against wickedness in high places, but simply a convenient cashing-in for the psychic currency of self-importance and elite attention? If true, how responsible was that?

GRADING WATERGATE

I am certain of one thing: When Richard Nixon's fight for political survival ended in a loss, it was a coalition of the unsavory and undeserving who got the win. Hypocritical partisan Democrats, allied with an activist liberal media and dedicated to policies that I knew would inevitably weaken America in the world and erode liberty at home, vaulted into the ascendancy as a result of Watergate in the elections of 1974 and 1976, one brief cycle after the Republican landslide of 1972. Being on their side for even a short time felt wrong to me then. It feels even more wrong as I look back.

My miniscule contribution was never going to weigh appreciably in the scale of how things turned out. But if responsible action is measured by outcomes, and if the outcome for which I cast my lot was to the country's detriment, maybe I don't even get a passing grade, let alone a stellar mark, for responsibility in that instance.

All right. Having now talked around the question from all sides—should I have resisted the scandal sooner and harder, or should I have taken the counsel of Ray Price and other wise elders and hung in to the end, or did I do pretty much the right thing at the right time—I won't take refuge in moral agnosticism here. The episode comes out as a B in my gradebook, on somewhat the same logic as my B in choosing a mate. I did act responsibly if hesitantly. But the old tentativeness was still there. An earlier and more decisive commitment would have earned a higher mark.

The fall of Nixon—like our country's Vietnam intervention and endgame, our slow-motion awakening to the threat of Islamic jihad, and our Iraq and Afghanistan interventions and endgame today— shows the deep ambivalence that often surrounds great events in the lives of nations. Personal accountability in our own lives can be similarly clouded, as I have just tried to illustrate.

In the crucible of Watergate, I largely went with what I felt. So did the country, taking its lead from how the Washington political and media elites felt. On balance, for the nation and for me, the outcome was a step toward truer responsibility. Yet it was a mixed and troubling outcome all the same. Once Americans learned of the "cancer on the presidency" about which John Dean had warned, it had to be removed, and it was. But deeper poisons remained in the body politic, even with Nixon gone and a number of his men convicted.

An unconscious rationalization that sometimes the end justifies the means—insidious irresponsibility indeed—was actually strengthened at the highest levels of power as a result of Watergate. As so often in politics or in our personal lives, the resolution of one difficult challenge only sets the stage for the next. Slow learner John Andrews would encounter that lesson again in years to come.

CHAPTER 10

MISSED OPPORTUNITIES

I Timothy 2:1, 2

D oing the right thing, doing our part, doing our best, doing what
we should and not just what we want—these shorthand expressions have stood as my rough definition for responsible living in the
book thus far. They are fine as a rule of thumb. But as usual the devil
is in the details.

I hope this report-card exercise is helping us see that personal
responsibility in real life is more nuanced and complex. Responsibility
has to weigh contradictory or competing claims. It can be approxi-
mated but never perfectly realized. Its ideal shape and balance are seldom clear until after the fact. Such is the human condition.

STEADY SELF-SCRUTINY

"I kept belatedly seeing my full responsibility," says the scribbled heading on my notes for this chapter. The same could be said of America
through the centuries. My report card on myself and yours on yourself, as well as the report card we might draw up on our nation's still-
unfinished experiment in responsible freedom, justly stamp all of us
as slow learners. That's not a stigma, however, but simply a birthmark.
We need to be patient with ourselves about it, though never compla-
cent. Steady self-scrutiny is part of the answer.

I would draw further examples from my stormy personal life around age 40, if this were an autobiography. It's not, so I won't. Suffice to say that in turning from the Christian Science faith that had meant everything for a hundred years to the Andrews and to Donna's family, the D'Evelyns—and later in passing through the nightmare of being divorced from her, prior to remarrying each other within the same year—I saw into the depth of my own selfishness with sickening clarity.

From the distance of 30 years, I can see that my motivations in both these crises, as in the Watergate episode, were a tangle of worse and better. But the outcome was a shattering of the illusion that it was "all about me." It was necessary for me to lose, for a time, not only what I thought I knew of God but also the affection and trust of loved ones God had blessed me with, in order at last to have those relationships reborn when meekness replaced my arrogance. (Or began to replace it; I'm afraid that remains a work in progress.)[37]

Are there analogies in our country's history for these searing metaphors of purgatory and redemption, death and rebirth? With reflection we could probably think of some. I believe it would be good to try.

MARKING THE 1990 RACE

Back to the public and political side of a slow learner's report card. What was my grade for responsibility in the doomed crusade of Andrews for Governor 1990? We've seen how I stepped forward— "Send me"[38]—when others hung back, similar to my plunge in the Watergate episode. We've seen how term limits and tax limits came to be enacted as guardrails against over-government in Colorado, as a result of my candidacy. The Independence Institute gained stature. A template was established for the unapologetically conservative governorship of Bill Owens eight years later. High marks might seem to be in order.

Then again, maybe not. Also as in Watergate, one could argue that in order to make a real difference—and not merely a gesture—with this ambitious for statewide office by a newcomer, I ought to have started earlier and prepared better, or otherwise held back and awaited the next wave. All the more so as unlike the other situation, there would be a next wave, and a next one after that. This was not a crisis; it was just another quadrennial election.

Wasn't your timing impulsive and irresponsible, John, setting aside the adrenaline factor and the quixotic impulse?[39] Judging by fact not fantasy, logic not emotion, one is tempted to agree.

Opportunity cost is not just economists' jargon. It's a law of nature. Resources committed here are unavailable to use over there, where the rate of return might have been double. "Sorry, you made your choice," says reality, sometimes to our regret. I do not regret that 1990 campaign; but in retrospect, I can see the opportunity cost.

My half-year of living dangerously as the sacrificial lamb against Bomber-Jacket Roy Romer had a high price in donated dollars, supporters' time and goodwill, and media characterization of my party and myself. It tagged me for better or worse with a distinct reputation among fellow Republicans (good try but bad loss) as well as among voters across the state (boy sent to do a man's job, and perhaps something of an extremist at that).[40]

In terms of best using your talents and serving your cause, John, mightn't it have been more responsible to play the long game and run when you were really ready? As an untried candidate at 46, going for all the marbles statewide, what was so urgent about 1990?

Maybe it was again more "about me" than I realized. Maybe that's why waiting until 1994 or 1998, 2002 or 2006 didn't occur to me. (In 2006, I would still have been only 62, exactly Romer's age when he won in 1990.)

With the benefit of two decades' hindsight, I find all this quite persuasive, uncomfortable though it is to admit. In a way, that campaign was my own little Vietnam, my Iraq—well intended but ill considered, in no way ignoble at the outset, carried off honorably enough under the circumstances, but highly problematic in cost-benefit terms at the end of the day.[41]

If responsibility were graded on the curve, Republican gubernatorial nominee Andrews might get an A for idealism and gumption and scrappiness, for sweeping the convention and making some good speeches and landing a few punches in the debates. But that's not how we're grading here, as I have explained. The responsible American is marked against the gold standard. By which criterion I mark that exam a D or C-. You knew better, boy. Or you should have.

SENATE SCOREBOARD

Let's take my six years in the Colorado Senate as our final case study. My earlier lessons in personal responsibility through the decades, some gained easily but many the hard way, should have prepared me to earn higher marks this time. The "Old Man," as military units call their commanding officer, was now really old enough to provide seasoned, sure-handed leadership in the battles our side faced. How did it play out?

The answer depends on who you think "our side" was, and what a winning outcome would look like. The scoreboard looked one way if it was just a matter of the Republicans taking more seats than the Democrats on the first Tuesday in November, or the conservatives passing this bill and defeating that one, or such and such a message dominating the news. The scoreboard looked very different if it was a matter of which ideas and values were gaining strength in our state, on a deeper level and toward a longer horizon.

My record for 1999-2005 certainly improved upon 1990. The senator who was, did better in obvious ways than the governor who never was. I fault myself again, however, for failing to "play the long game." I made too many gambles and too few alliances. I listened too little and hurried too much. I scanned the surface when I should have probed the unseen. I improvised when I should have strategized.

The Senate District 27 vacancy race in 1998 went in my favor despite an eleventh-hour decision to run. It was rather like any number of peaks I've climbed, 10K races I've done, or speeches I've given—successful with a minimum of preparation. Caught again by the paradox where responsibility enables success and success then erodes responsibility, I came into the Senate with the self-imposed disadvantage of no big vision for how to make the most of the opportunity. A year of planning and forethought, ahead of my one-month sprint for the open seat, could have readied me to be far more strategic for the goals that really matter.

What might those goals have been? They would have related to advancing Element R. At that time, a decade ago, the nonpartisan responsibility movement in America was far along, even as the conservative political movement was starting to lose headway. I didn't do the hard thinking and patient study to see that. So I missed the chance to orient my whole time in the Senate around a responsibility theme. Only later did I recognize the road not taken. There is no regret or self-reproach in this. The report card has to reflect it, though.

I now believe it is possible for elected officials to legislate, communicate, network, and campaign in ways that help renew our civic health by fostering citizen responsibility. But that is so far outside the contemporary norm that it won't happen unless taken as a conscious and determined objective. It was not an objective of mine as a senator because I had not equipped myself with the necessary tools.

For this reason, while there is satisfaction in my legislative aspirations and accomplishments as tallied earlier, they can't receive the highest grade for responsible stewardship of power. In our private lives, Americans bear various kinds of responsibility—familial, vocational, legal, moral, and so forth. But winning an election and taking an oath raises the stakes. In accepting a public trust, we step up to an added level of obligation that might be called "personal responsibility for communal responsibility."

This means that by one's own example and exercise of power, he either strengthens or weakens the responsibility ethic as it applies to individuals and institutions in our society as a whole. During my time as a representative of Senate District 27, I instinctively knew this and did my best to live up to it. With conscious awareness, however, I could have exercised much greater personal responsibility for communal responsibility. If only, as the saying goes, I knew then what I know now.

This is one of the most important points I hope to convey in these pages. Abstractions and generalities cannot convey it. In the closing chapters, I will give many specific examples of the concept, with recommendations for our nation going forward. For now, consider its application to the Senator from Backbone.

COLORADO LOST GROUND

What if I had taken office with a determination to see the responsibility ethic more fully honored in Colorado's public policies and political culture? At least one member out of the 35 in our chamber would be answering roll call each day with the unstated but unswerving mission to act as the Senator from Element R. My conservative ideology and Republican loyalty, though undiminished, would now be means to that end, not ends in themselves. Would it have made a difference? I think so.

The bottom line is that our state today is one where government does significantly *more* for individuals, and individuals do significantly *less* for themselves, than was the case when I was a new senator 12 years ago. The responsibility ethic has lost ground. It was not defended faithfully enough and skillfully enough by me and others who claimed allegiance to it. Clearly we needed to do more.

Taxes, spending, regulation, entitlements, education, health, energy, transportation, corrections, bureaucracy, unionization, litigation—in these and other areas of public policy, Colorado continues toward a collectivized approach and away from the old responsible standard, "It's up to you. Choose and take the consequences." Our Republican party has in some cases supported this by acts of commission. We have allowed it in other cases by acts of omission, among them a string of election losses. Along the way I've earned many scars as a fighting conservative, but to what benefit?

The grade for my Senate years would be higher if I had paid more attention to relationships and less to electoral scalps—if I had led the way in talking common sense with Coloradans while keeping the Republican and conservative brand in the background. All of this is just another way of saying I thought too little about playing the long game.

Better led during the spring sessions and the summer campaigns, our Senate caucus could have done better at the fall elections than 17 Republicans in 2000, 18 in 2002, and 17 again in 2004. I wasn't the only leader in those cycles, but I was one of them, and a large share of responsibility for the mediocrity is mine. Working more shrewdly with the moderates in both parties, with business allies, with the media, we needn't have lost the Senate two out of four times while Owens was governor.[42] A string of bad bills and bad ballot issues, the Referendum C tax increase of 2005 worst among them, would not be law today.

Some of the controversial and confrontational legislation that put me in the media spotlight now seems, with the perspective of time, a distraction from the greater priorities of incremental change, structural reform, and playing the percentages for electoral success. My judicial term limits proposals of 1999 and 2004, my Ten Commandments bill of 2000 in response to Columbine the year before, and especially my hubris with the redistricting bill of 2003, were not great moments in statesmanship. Responsibility and the self-indulgent gesture don't mix; here too I've not been the quickest learner.

Backbone had a senator under Colorado's gold dome for a few years. It has a blogger now. Fair enough. Element R didn't have a senator when it needed one, though. At least it didn't have me, and that's too bad, because with more forethought going in and more discernment along the way, it might have.

So mark down the 1999-2005 record as acceptable but average. The exam wasn't blown. We had no debacles or disasters, blunders or betrayals. But the missed opportunities were many, and the responsibility ethic suffered as a result. Final grade for my Senate years: C+.

EVEN SLOW LEARNERS LEARN

Let's take a minute to review and sum up. My wife Donna says that the big turkey dinner she makes for Thanksgiving always tastes better to her as leftovers the next day. Only on Friday does the cook and hostess get to savor what was hurried onto the plates for Thursday's hungry guests. Our two sittings with my political life story in these pages have been a little bit like that. We went through once for events and color, then more reflectively again for self-appraisal. Filling out my report card was no picnic, yet it has been a feast of discovery for me with many garnishes of gratitude as well as a few of regret. Thanksgiving itself is that way, haven't you found?

The responsibility report card covered big events including a crisis of conscience in the White House, a long-shot run for Governor, and a season in the Colorado Senate, along with smaller personal tests to broaden the behavioral sample. For each test I assigned a grade as objectively as I could. My lifetime GPA, self-marked, comes out somewhere between a C and a B.

Another examiner might mark me lower or higher. That doesn't matter a lot. The honest discipline of doing a report card, first on ourselves as a baseline, and then on our country, is more important than what the score turns out to be. The key is responsible introspection.

It's needed because we're all learners in the world's classroom, and slow learners at that. The Andrews chronicle is relevant only as a case study in how the classroom works. My ethical biopsy is charted here not because very many people care about it as such, but in hope of starting a conversation about America's responsibility ethic—getting us to think together about where the responsibility ethic healthy and where it may need some healing.

You'll remember the rueful confession a few pages ago: "I kept belatedly seeing my full responsibility." You'll also remember the warnings of decline from Glubb and Tytler, suggesting that irresponsibility fed by success eventually besets all great nations. And you'll remember my question:

What analogy can we draw between one slow-learning American of the Boomer Generation, and America's own collective loss and rebirth of responsibility in these times?

I speculated whether the report card on myself could become a template for a report card on my country. I believe in fact it can, and here's why. The thing about slow learners is that they do learn. Individuals don't just age and stiffen. They also deepen and toughen. They slow but they also grow. As they endure, they mature. The seasons season them. Their selfishness has a chance to drop away. It may not, but there is the chance. A person may then age out of smallness into bigness. Gradually, painfully, even most dullards get it .

Sir John Glubb warned us

Though my life transcript hardly shows a dramatic uptrend toward the perfect 4.0, and though foresight remains poorer than hindsight even now, the overall trajectory is toward contributing more unselfishly, becoming more accountable and self-aware. It can be said, I hope, that the very act of writing a responsibility report card instead of a Backbone manifesto is responsible in a way you'd never have seen from the brash young Johnnie A.

America as a free and responsible society, structured to give scope to the individual as no other society ever has, possesses to an unusual degree the same capacity that individuals possess for growth in accompaniment with aging, self-renewal in defiance of decline. The idealism of our heritage and the openness of our institutions give rise to ceaseless self-criticism and self-correction—an immense advantage over the more rigid and fatalistic societies elsewhere on the globe or at earlier periods in history.

This parallels, on a national scale, the same constructively discontented spirit I've tried to illustrate with personal stories. It has made itself felt throughout our country, over the roughly the same period as my adult life, in the responsibility movement, Element R. It operates as a sort of moral antibody to counteract the declinist forces diagnosed by Glubb and Tytler.

As I have a good bit of life left to live, God willing, there will be more entries on my responsibility transcript, many private ones and perhaps some public ones as well. What's logged here is only the record to date. Likewise, the gradebook is still open on responsible America and the remnant. Our marks in the nation's third century, 1976 to the present, are not bad so far.

A slow-learning America seems to be learning that success doesn't license irresponsibility. We are awakening to the seduction of the paradox and rousing ourselves. Our responsibility deficit, alarming not so long ago, is being repaired. A decade of decision is now upon us, Part Three will show.

PART THREE

RESPONSIBILITIES

CHAPTER 11

WHEN THINGS
WERE DARKEST

Matthew 7:26, 27

We now turn back from one citizen's self-scrutiny to the broader question of every citizen's responsibility as a new century accelerates. I call to the witness stand a prophetic voice expelled from the enemy camp to seek asylum in ours: Alexander Solzhenitsyn. Understanding us perhaps better than we understood ourselves, he gave a testimony of truth deserving our deepest consideration.

Remember, responsible America was founded on self-evident truths. Good and evil, right and wrong, reality and illusion, were understood to be objective and knowable. Obligation and duty were rooted in natural law. Doing what you should was common sense. It followed from human nature. The responsibility ethic matched logically with what everyone knew to be true about *Homo sapiens*.

But that was then. Eight, nine, ten generations along from the heroic age of the Founders, thought-leaders in our country had come to regard the very concept of truth as passé. There was no clearer sign that we were a civilization in trouble.

Take Harvard University. Its proud motto *Veritas*, Latin for "truth", held mocking irony as the American bicentennial came on. The institution's weighty influence was invariably allied to that suave relativism which dismisses truth, along with goodness, as subjective if not illusory. An historic exception occurred, though, when Solzhenitsyn was invited to speak at Harvard on June 8, 1978.

WOUNDS OF A FRIEND

The Russian literary giant had been living in Vermont since 1974. The Soviet regime hated his dissident writings, yet feared the consequences of returning him to the Gulag where his electrifying first novel, *One Day in the Life of Ivan Denisovich*, had originated. They exiled him instead. Shamefully, a weak Gerald Ford had refused to receive the great man at the White House in 1975. Laudably, Harvard now lent its prestige to Solzhenitsyn's truth-telling, midway through the even weaker presidency of Jimmy Carter.

Solzhenitsyn has long been one of my heroes. History will rank him as one of the greatest men of the past hundred years. His death in August 2008 helped inspire me to write this book. As Marxist-Leninist communism is the ultimate negation of personal responsibility and

Bitter truth from Solzhenitsyn

the Christian faith is among the highest expressions of personal responsibility, Solzhenitsyn's compelling witness for the one and against the other earns him an honored place in these pages.

The Harvard Class Day address is easily found in his collected writings or on the Internet. It is a document that every educated American should know. The Russian's somber warning to his U.S. hosts exemplifies the proverb of Solomon: "Faithful are the wounds of a friend."[43]

The intellectual priesthood heard a searing account of America's responsibility deficit on that day in 1978, whether they liked it or not. Most did not. The choices and challenges still before us, as well as the symptoms of our malaise, had never been painted more vividly. Alexander Solzhenitsyn's diagnosis and prescription, delivered three decades ago when things were darkest, can serve us today as a baseline for measuring what has been done since then about those challenges, and what must now be done in this decisive decade.

MORAL POVERTY

"Truth seldom is pleasant; it is almost invariably bitter," Solzhenitsyn began. But friendship was the motive for any bitterness in what would follow on this occasion, the visitor added. His assessment of the condition of America and the West was severe. He saw us as being in "a state of psychological weakness," "moral poverty," and "spiritual exhaustion." Leadership elites showed "depression, passivity, and perplexity." In this climate, it would "sound simply absurd" to urge "self-restraint… sacrifice, and selfless risk."[44]

Our country and our civilization, he observed, had been softened by "habitual extreme safety and well-being [which] are not advantageous for a living organism." Echoes of Glubb and Tytler rang in this warning, and in the Russian's question: "Should one point out that from ancient times a decline in courage has been considered the beginning of the end?"[45]

In the Harvard address, as in all his writings, the prophetic Solzhenitsyn was not unfailingly prescient. Events since 1976 have *not* borne out his dark musings that "the next war… may well bury Western civilization forever" or that "the Western way of life is less and less likely to become the leading model" for emulation around the world.[46] However this does not justify ignoring him as a cranky doomsayer. Too much of his analysis rings grim and true, as when he states that "between the freedom to do good and the freedom to do evil," we have established inequality in favor of the latter. He gives this illustration:

> Life organized legalistically has thus shown its inability to defend itself against the corrosion of evil…. When a government starts an earnest fight against terrorism, public opinion immediately accuses it of violating the terrorists' civil rights.[47]

Sound familiar? Remember, this was a year before the Tehran hostages were seized and 23 years before the September 11 attacks by jihadists on US soil. The slow but steady fulfillment of his warnings almost makes them more impressive, not less. Perhaps this author who gave us *August 1914* and the other documentary novels in his Red Wheel cycle could see as far and as perceptively into the future as he did into the past. The apocalyptic tone in such pronouncements as the following, hokey though it may seem to shallow thinkers, may prove all too accurate in the fullness of time. Is there a "fight for our planet"? Solzhenitsyn thinks so:

> The fight, physical and spiritual, for our planet, a fight of cosmic proportions, is not a vague matter of the future. It has already started. The forces of Evil have begun their decisive offensive, you [in the West] can feel their pressure... [yet believing you] cannot apply moral criteria to politics... [you] make space for the absolute triumph of absolute evil in the world.[48]

The key words in this passage, the keys to Solzhenitsyn's diagnosis and prescription at Harvard, are "moral" and "spiritual." The West must replace its "moral mediocrity" with "moral responsibility" before it's too late, he told the Class Day audience. I have argued in these pages that America has since rallied in defiance of the odds and begun doing exactly that. Our country's victory in the Cold War—which the Russian prophet despite his worst fears lived to see, even being repatriated to his homeland with honor in 1994 and later running for president—was therefore in some degree his doing.

On the other hand, the cosmic struggle he discerned between good and evil did not end with the end of the Soviet Union. Solzhenitsyn makes clear in the concluding section of the Harvard address that he sees beliefs, attitudes, and worldviews, not material factors such as politics and economics, as decisive for mankind's future in the coming centuries. And he paints on a giant canvas: the Middle Ages, the Renaissance, the Enlightenment, and now modernity. The worst "disaster" of the latter, he says, has been "the calamity of a despiritualized and irreligious humanistic consciousness."[49]

Here let me pause the discussion, personally inject John Andrews, and establish a key point. I am a religious man, a follower of Jesus Christ, and I would not know how to be anything else. But this is not intended as a religious book. Emphatically not. On the contrary, this book aims to show how the responsibility ethic has historically provided and can continue providing a common ground of citizenship for Americans of differing religions and of no religion at all. That's why I believe we have much to learn from Solzhenitsyn's brief for responsibility as given in the 1978 oration. He makes a case that partakes of his own deep religiosity but is not confined by it. In the additional citations that follow, we see not only the great man's God-centered outlook, but also his inescapable challenge for less-devout Westerners to take stock and think anew within their own more pluralistic outlook.

LIFE OF DUTY

The Russian urged his Harvard audience to beware of the ominous "logic of materialistic development" set in motion by the West's "total liberation from [its] moral heritage," whereby the individual is left with "boundless freedom simply for the satisfaction of his whims or instincts." If you want to save yourselves, he told his hosts, "It is time, in the West, to defend not so much human rights as human obligations."[50]

People must learn again to see their "task on earth" as "the fulfillment of a permanent, earnest duty, so that one's life journey may become an experience of moral growth." As for how this would come about, Solzhenitsyn—knowing his audience—made no reference to deity or creeds but limited himself to saying, much in the same vein as Sir John Glubb's closing exhortation: "Only voluntarily inspired self-restraint can raise man above the strain of materialism."[51]

Voluntarily inspired self-restraint! Here was no slightest hint of the religious repression which some claim to fear from people of faith. The offset to his concern about a despiritualized consciousness turns out not to be coercive re-churching of the masses but personal re-spiritualizing of individuals—where the spiritual factor is understood as whatever tempers the animal selfishness of "imperfect man, who is never free of pride, self-interest, envy, vanity, and dozens of other defects." [52]

Compare the insistence by Glubb, quoted earlier, that "only a revival of spiritual devotion, not fashionable 'isms,' can inspire selfless service." [53] The British soldier and the Russian author, writing from profoundly different life experiences and within a couple of years of each other, chose nearly identical phrasing. Neither was suggesting a theocracy or anything like it. Both were getting at a deep truth about the human condition, a truth that most of the elites in America and Europe at that time did not want to face.

Could there be such a thing as excessively enforcing human rights? Solzhenitsyn at Harvard dared to say there was: "The West [since Locke and Rousseau] ended up by truly enforcing human rights, sometimes excessively, but man's sense of responsibility to God and society grew dimmer and dimmer.... On the way from the Renaissance to our days we... lost the concept of a Supreme Complete Entity which used to restrain our passions and our irresponsibility." [54]

At the nation's birth 1776, he pointed out, Americans had understood that "all individual human rights were granted because man is God's creature. That is, freedom was given to the individual conditionally, on the assumption of his constant religious responsibility." But now, "all such limitations were discarded"—an abandonment of responsibility unimaginable "even fifty years ago." [55]

NO WAY BUT UP

The perceptiveness of those words is evident if one looks back exactly half a century from Alexander Solzhenitsyn's speech in Cambridge to President Calvin Coolidge's address at Independence Hall on July 4, 1926—a landmark of political wisdom and moral rigor. [56] The question of how things could have slid so far, so fast, is what I wanted to frame by reviewing the Russian's jeremiad at length.

He did not have, nor claim, unerring foresight. His insight, though, read the times and called the moment better than anyone I know of. He described the moment this way: "If the world has not come to its end,"—and it hadn't; hear the irony, picture the self-mocking smile– "it has approached a major turn in history [which] will exact from us a spiritual upsurge[;] we shall have to rise to a new height of vision.... No one on earth has any way left but—upward."[57]

Those are the final words of Solzhenitsyn's Harvard Address, June 8, 1978. Opportunity was hinted in his peroration, but not as a path of roses. The upward path, if America had the fortitude to take it, would be steep and rugged. We know now that America summoned the fortitude and seized the opportunity. In the ensuing decades she began to find her way upward, showing other nations the way as well, doing her part toward realization of a "new height of vision" for everyone on earth.

I believe the spiritual upsurge our Russian friend looked for *is* occurring, in the form of a responsibility movement encompassing religious and non-religious impulses alike. I am also struck by the dimensional axis he chose—up or down, rather than left or right. This is a reminder that our political problems require moral solutions, now as then. It reaffirms the identical warning given by Ronald Reagan in 1964, and it points to the transpartisan inclusiveness that we hope to see today in Element R.[58]

The rebirth of responsibility is a continuing story for our nation and for each of us as citizens. To meet the opportunities of this next American century, we must be clear about how the responsibility deficit overtook us in the last century. How did we lose our way? Why didn't the old restraints hold? Where did the slide start and bottom out? What energized the turnaround? How complete is responsibility's comeback? What's the next crucial battle line? What dangers loom? We'll now tackle those questions.

CHAPTER 12

HOW WE LOST OUR WAY

Revelation 2:4

L ife is duty, Alexander Solzhenitsyn told the stunned Harvard dons. Freedom is conditional on responsibility, the Russian insisted, as you Americans once knew well. But you forgot it within a single lifetime, and now evil is gaining. This can't go on, he warned. We're at a turn in history. Upward is the only way out.

Solzhenitsyn's address was a testament for the ages and for our country's time of need. As a citizen's guide to the next American century, I could not improve on it. An hour of thunder from this giant comes to the same point as my dozen chapters of political reflection and personal memoir. A more profound point, really, because distilled from a greater soul.

My intention in offering a map for the decades ahead was never to attempt a crystal-ball exercise or compile an issues manual. Just the opposite. I'm contending, on the evidence of modern history and one citizen's observations, that moral factors will always and everywhere prove decisive. Integrity and character outweigh all. Times change, truth does not. Human nature does not.

The traps and temptations luring people away from responsibility don't change a lot either. So it is important for us to learn all we can from bitter experiences of the century past as a caution against repeating its mistakes. We can be forearmed today if we understand how irresponsibility seduced America in our parents' and grandparents' day. The responsibilities they shirked, we shall be equipped to fulfill.

AMERICA'S AFTERNOON

The low point our country reached in the 1970s, economically and politically adrift, morally and culturally mediocre, militarily drained, had been a long time coming. Solzhenitsyn spoke of the ebbing of responsibility across fifty years. Glubb dated the onset of America's afternoon somewhere before 1920. When a generation of tough-minded leaders and thinkers passed from the scene after the Anglo-American victory in World War I, time-honored conceptions of right and wrong passed with them.

The wisdom of Rudyard Kipling in his biting 1919 poem, "The Gods of the Copybook Headings," fell on deaf ears in the impatient postwar world.[59] Free men must not again by fooled by the faddish notions that "promised perpetual peace… but when we disarmed, they… delivered us bound to our foe," wrote the sage old bard of the British Empire. So what, the optimists shrugged. When Kipling in the same poem sounded the time-tested warnings that two and two make four, all that glitters isn't gold, fire will always burn us and water make us wet, young minds in a hurry thought they knew better.

On this side of the Atlantic, the verities preached by stern conservatives like Calvin Coolidge were likewise ignored by the rising men of both parties. Neither the followers of Republican technocrat Herbert Hoover nor those of Democratic visionary Franklin Roosevelt paid much heed when President Coolidge, speaking at Philadelphia on the 150th anniversary of the Declaration of Independence, asserted:

> In my opinion, very little of just criticism can attach to the theories and principles of our institutions. There is far more danger of harm than there is hope of good in any radical changes..... Our forefathers came to certain conclusions... which have been a great blessing to the world....We must think the thoughts which they thought. Their intellectual life… was not so much engrossed in how much they knew, or how much they had, as in how they were going to live.[60]

To live well, as I have repeatedly urged, must be to live by the responsibility ethic. Coolidge—like the Founders—understood this in a way that the liberal icon FDR never did. Notice how Coolidge's thought anticipates that of Solzhenitsyn, in the closing lines from the same 1926 speech:

> We live in an age of science and of abounding accumulation of material things. These did not create our Declaration. Our Declaration created them. The things of the spirit come first. Unless we cling to that, all our material prosperity, overwhelming though it may appear, will turn to a barren sceptre in our grasp. If we are to maintain the great heritage which has been bequeathed to us, we must be like-minded as the fathers who created it. We must not sink into a pagan materialism. We must cultivate the reverence which they had for the things that are holy. We must follow the spiritual and moral leadership which they showed.[61]

I am suggesting that responsible America is defined by forever doing things the same or always thinking the same. Innovation in itself is not irresponsible, obviously not. Irresponsibility is the hubris or utopianism that believes it can shortcut the laws of the universe.

That's what tough-minded thinkers such as Coolidge and Kipling were trying to head off as the 1920s roared into the "low, dishonest decade" of the '30s.[62]

Coolidge: Spirit comes first

Responsibility nurturing success, then success suffocating responsibility, the paradox we keep encountering, overtook the United States in the first third of the 20th century. Victorious, Americans refused to remain engaged with Europe or stay prepared for war. Prosperous, they rode an economic bubble to ruin. Frightened into collectivism, they let a recession become the Depression. But to note all this is still to describe only symptoms, not causes. The causes lay much deeper, in the moral dry-rot and carelessness of character identified by Tytler and Glubb.

Then in the middle third of the 20th century, the unraveling continued but took a different form. Our parents, justly called the Greatest Generation for their heroism in the public square, were irresolute at the home hearth. They wanted to spare their children from the privations they had faced in hard times and wartime. In parenting the Baby Boomers—my generation—they acted as if sacrifice and all the Spartan virtues could now be made optional.

Never did good intentions pave a more hellish road. Outmoded notions such as defeating enemies, stopping subversives, or punishing criminals were replaced by softer substitutes. Carelessness of character worsened until the pampered young threw a national tantrum in the 1960s. University intellectuals and imperious judges, clever enough to cow the common sense of Main Street, were no match for the baby boomers' raging resentment. They folded spinelessly.

Authority had become a laughingstock. The idea of responsibility no longer meant personal duty and grateful obligation; it was inverted into a weapon of mass indictment. Life became a blame game where everything was someone else's fault. Religion faltered with self-doubt. Liberty had degraded to license in the land of the free. "Tune in, turn on, drop out." "Make love, not war." "Burn, baby, burn." "Off the pigs." "Trust no one over 30." "God is dead." What a time.

GRAVE SYMPTOMS

The erosion of America's responsibility ethic occurred gradually and quietly. But the process surged in three episodes, each showing the temptation to irresponsibility under a different face.

- During the presidencies of Theodore Roosevelt and Woodrow Wilson, progressivism centralized expectations around a messianic leader and fostered a cult of the new.

- In the 1930s, fear so demoralized civil society that political manipulation of the economy was welcomed as never before.

■ And finally in the '60s, the delirium of "affluenza" exploded into narcissism, romanticism, indulgence, rebellion, and a glorification of the irrational.

The responsibility deficit, worsening over several decades, had reached a crisis point by the time of Lyndon Johnson and Richard Nixon. Looking back from the election of Jimmy Carter in 1976 to that of William McKinley 1900 (with Theodore Roosevelt as his running mate), we notice grave symptoms emerging. All sorts of key indicators had moved in the wrong direction as the century wore on. Dependency on government was up. Promiscuity, illegitimacy, and divorce were up. Crime and drug abuse were up. Black poverty was up.[63] Family stability and childbearing were down. Academic standards were down and educators were disrespected. The warrior spirit was down and soldiers were spat upon.

Self-government through the democratic process had atrophied as judicial lawmaking grew. Mothers were licensed to take their unborn babies' lives by the millions as a result. God was all but unmentionable in the public square as another result. Patriotism was apologetic. Merit was suspect. Colleges were leftist and lax. Popular entertainment was debased. Cultural confidence was shaken. Debt soared and saving fell.

The essentials of citizenship in our Republic, understood by thoughtful statesmen from John Adams to John Kennedy, practiced by Americans for two centuries, suddenly seemed indefensible or inoperative. JFK's assassination may have extinguished them entirely, some speculated.[64]

Those essentials are four, according to Prof. Thomas Krannawitter, as you will recall: Self-assertion, self-restraint, self-reliance, and civic knowledge. Sixties culture enlightened us on how backward all this was, however. Civic knowledge would now equate to a catechism of America's unforgivable sins. Victimhood and entitlement replaced self-reliance. Grievance obviated self-restraint. And only the oppressed could now assert themselves. From the alleged oppressor class, self-abasement in perpetuity was demanded—although it could never expunge their guilt.

With this for a citizen's guide, circa 1969—as Martin Luther King and Robert Kennedy had now also been martyred, as buses ringed the White House while radical students marched for defeat in Vietnam and Walter Cronkite pronounced the war unwinnable—there seemed little likelihood of another American century. And a good thing, said the reigning irresponsibles. One American century was one too many, in their view.[65]

LUCE AND TOCQUEVILLE

Yet we must not fail to recognize that despite all the trends and traumas I have described here, old Henry Luce was absolutely right in characterizing the 20th century as the American century. Up to the 1950s, it had been exactly that. So resilient is our open society with its self-critical and self-correcting genius, so potent is freedom as a resource for human achievement, that we had been able to accomplish immense good for ourselves and for the world even as our tendency to irresponsibility mounted.

Any deficit eventually takes its toll, however. By the 1970s, personal responsibility seemed so weakened that the relationship between citizens and their government was approaching the dystopian condition imagined long ago by Alexis de Tocqueville. The Frenchman worried in 1840 about the rise of

> an immense and tutelary power, which takes upon itself alone to secure [the people's] gratifications and to watch over their fate.... [indeed almost] to spare them all the care of thinking and all the trouble of living[.] Thus it every day renders the exercise of the free agency of man less useful and less frequent; it... gradually robs a man of all the usefulness of himself.[66]

This benignly oppressive regime is no despotic tyranny, no enemy of the people, Tocqueville explains: "For their happiness such a government willingly labors." It is "provident and mild," ruling by their ready consent, because the spirit of the age—an equality principle that deadens community and mutual obligation—"has prepared men for these things; it has predisposed men to endure them as benefits." As a result:

> The will of man is not shattered, but softened, bent, and guided; men are seldom forced by [government] to act, but they are constantly restrained from acting. Such a power does not destroy, but it prevents existence; it does not tyrannize, but it compresses, enervates, extinguishes, and stupefies a people, till [the] nation is reduced to nothing better than a flock of timid and industrious animals of whom the government is the shepherd.[67]

How does a nation become something other than itself? How is a heritage lost? How does freedom die? When responsibility dies first. That's what I take from these chilling passages in *Democracy in America*, so similar to the insights of Tytler, Glubb, and Solzhenitsyn.

THE SHEEP AWAKEN

But in the years since that low point of the 1970s, neither responsibility nor freedom died, thank God. Americans proved themselves to be no flock of timid sheep. The fighting spirit of "Don't tread on me" still lived. A moral awakening, similar in some ways to the religious awakenings that had preceded the Revolutionary War and the Civil War, stirred the land.

We have seen how the responsible remnant arose as a result. Conservative politics was but one facet of a many-sided national renewal. Among the earliest and most powerful forces in responsibility's rebirth were aspirations now commonly identified with liberalism and Democrats. Civil rights was one. Opportunity for women was another. Environmental stewardship was another.

Ideology and party would complicate—or clarify—these matters later on. At the outset, wherever you saw individuals being empowered to choose and take the consequences; wherever you saw communities embracing mutual obligation; there you saw the remnant, responsible America on the comeback trail.

The comeback was personified in some ways by Ronald Reagan, electrifying Republicans with his primary challenge to Gerald Ford in 1976 before sweeping to the White House in 1980, insisting government was the problem not the answer, confronting the Evil Empire, invoking the city on a hill.

But neither party engineered the comeback. Rather it re-engineered the parties, both of them, in significant ways. Jimmy Carter and the Democratic Congress, deregulating airlines and trucking, cutting capital gains taxes, were part of responsibility's rebirth. The same was seen when Carter hit the Soviets with an Olympic boycott after they raped Afghanistan. Not grand statecraft, perhaps, but would any president since JFK have done as much? I doubt it. America herself was beginning to change just then. Leaders across the board had to scramble to keep up.

Both parties had helped worsen the responsibility deficit. Both would now have a role in repairing it. Victory in the Cold War, Reagan's supreme achievement, could not have come without the contributions of such Democrats as Scoop Jackson, Jeane Kirkpatrick, Norman Podhoretz, and Daniel Patrick Moynihan. President Bill Clinton signed welfare reform. Senator Joe Lieberman stood by President George W. Bush on Iraq.

Responsible America is not Republican or Democratic America, as I have tried to make clear from the outset. Responsible America is not conservative or liberal America. It is the America of character and integrity, moral realism and spiritual humility—the America that cares passionately about right and wrong.

Not otherwise could we have been so evenly divided over the last five presidential elections, neither party dominant, and still felt ourselves getting stronger and saner as a country all along. The reason is responsibility reborn, the sensible center toward which both parties must gravitate in order to compete.

It's a mistake, regardless, to define the comeback of responsibility in purely political terms, or to identify it too closely with presidents and other personalities. Governance and policy did not set the trend. They followed along with it. The struggle was fought out in the American psyche, or if you prefer, the American soul.

'THIS IS WRONG'

Attitudes spiraled downward for many years into softness and immaturity, alternately petulant or dreamy, reckless or cowering. Tytler, or whoever he was, foretold the whole sequence. But then, remarkably, as Glubb hoped and urged, we the people began to sober up and grow up. Backbone stiffened and conscience stirred. "This is wrong." "This is foolish." "This is shameful." "This is unworthy of us." "We're better than this." "If not us, who? If not now, when?" One heart and one mind at a time, things turned. Change-agents then began to confront each of the '60s and '70s pathologies spelled out above.

Today, a third of the way into the next American century, is the responsibility ethic being lived out to the fullest in our country? Hardly. But active effort has replaced passivity in so many areas. Agitation for higher standards has replaced fatalism and mediocrity. Churches show a vitality unimaginable 40 years ago. The abortion license remains in law, but moral consensus has shifted against it. Charter schools, parental choice, and home schooling have put teacher unions on the defensive. Unionism in general has faded as worker self-determination grew.

The family, bulwark of responsible America, remains a beleaguered institution. Yet many Baby Boomers' children and grandchildren, damaged by the divorce epidemic, now seek to break the cycle. US birthrates are well above those of dying Europe. Optimism and altruism are stronger on this side of the Atlantic. US charitable giving is evidence of the same.

Crime is off nationally; New York led the way. Doing drugs stopped being cool. Serving in uniform began to be—a reversal from 1971 when John Kerry threw away his medals. Today our armed forces not only win their wars, they are also the nation's proudest equal-opportunity institution.

Other authors have chronicled the data and the dynamics of these encouraging changes in the past generation with more detail than I'll provide here. One of the best accounts is by Michael Barone in his book, *Hard America, Soft America: Competition vs. Coddling and the Battle for the Nation's Future* (New York, 2004).

Barone's title points to the obvious reality that our national toughening-up, the rebirth of responsibility, has been uneven in its results and is still a work in process. The battle for the nation's future, already assumed lost by some in Ford and Carter days, has turned encouragingly in the remnant's favor since then. But there is still a lot to be done, and the battle continues.

The Barone framework of competition versus coddling can help us think more clearly about past and future battles. Shielding individuals or institutions from the consequences of bad choices does them an awful disservice. Look at it in terms of the essentials of citizenship, cited previously from Thomas Krannawitter. When I'm coddled, my self-reliance languishes. Why bother, it's a free ride. My self-assertion can go over the top and my self-restraint gets the day off. No penalty either way.

Continuing in the same vein, with a couple of related qualities Krannawitter didn't highlight: When I'm coddled my self-improvement checks out and my self-respect sags. This creates a void that no amount of "self-esteem" cheerleading can fill.

Whereas if you cut the apron strings and make me compete, all those debilitating effects are avoided. Citizens and their voluntary communities are spared the paternalism that Tocqueville said "enervates, extinguishes, and stupefies" people, keeping them "in a perpetual state of childhood." Instead of that downward spiral, a positive feedback process takes hold. Self-restraint liberates self-reliance, which in turn empowers self-assertion.

Society works better when incentives are naturally aligned. Enterprise is rewarded and excess is checked. Civic knowledge reveals a political and economic order approximating justice and dignity, not a rigged game or a stifling kindergarten. All this when there is less coddling and more competition.

Striking the balance is still not easy, and reasonable people can differ. Compassion isn't the same as coddling. Competition can sometimes be cruel. Michael Barone, always thoughtful and incisive, has written a book, not a bumper sticker. He skillfully navigates these complexities, as readers will find.

PARTING WAYS

Allowing for nuances, I believe the dichotomy in Barone's title goes far to explain how responsibility came to be reborn. It also hints at "the rest of the story" on how some early contributors to the rebirth veered over into political opposition after a time.

We noted three of those: the movements for civil rights, for women's opportunity, and for environmental stewardship. Initially the logic was crystal clear. Keeping individuals down for any reason, treating them as an underclass, denies them personal responsibility even as it violates freedom and equality. Nor is it responsible to foul our nest, heedless of the harm to neighbors and descendants. Irresponsible arrogance and hubris discredit such behaviors. American conscience, belatedly like a slow learner, began repudiating those behaviors starting in the 1950s.

"This is wrong. We can do better," citizens started telling each other. Moral clarity took us that far. Those years of deeper national self-scrutiny were a proud chapter in that American century—and a glimpse into the next century. Then the tone changed. Minority suffering was said to prove majority guilt. Feminist idealism was held to justify antisocial anger. Earth was termed the goddess Gaia and humans a cancer upon her.

Victimhood triumphed. Whites, males, Christians, capitalist prosperity, and Western civilization itself, victimizers all, must pay. Only government command and control could set things right. Personal responsibility was inadequate at best, oppressors' propaganda at worst, according to this neo-Marxist critique.

The responsible remnant, committed to sensible care of the environment then, now, and always, committed to "all created equal," had no choice but to part ways politically with the special-interest pressure groups that swung far left of center as the storm of grievance rose.

It's sad. It didn't have to be that way. By radicalizing, those elements opted themselves out of Element R with its mainstream commitment to repairing the responsibility deficit. The rest of us could either grant their irresponsible agenda of punishment and plunder, favoritism and privilege—or we could resist that agenda and work toward becoming a more competitive, less coddling America—responsible America. We couldn't do both. Thus far the second course has narrowly prevailed.

Steady good sense and the quiet heroism of millions have brought our country a long ways, against the odds, in responsibility's amazing comeback since the 1970s. It's a great time to be alive. Now comes the decade of decision.

CHAPTER 13

WHAT MUST BE DONE

Matthew 22:21

Like the century behind us, the next American century will be a do-it-yourself experience. As citizens, we are crew members, not passengers, on this voyage of responsibility and freedom. Other nations that are defined by blood or soil may roll on from generation to generation by their own momentum. But our nation, defined by ideas, "dedicated to a proposition," depends constantly on you and me to sustain it.

All that America really is—or ever was—is a commonly-agreed set of ideas about God, man, truth, good, and government. The consensus has never been unanimous, and it is certainly less solid today than it was a generation ago. But this is our heritage, our birthright, and it must be constantly defended. If we neglect that moral and intellectual defense, America will soon become unrecognizable. So, the future of our country is our responsibility—because the future of responsibility is our responsibility.

"What is required of us now is a new era of responsibility." When President Barack Obama gave that challenge in his inaugural address on January 20, 2009, I initially cheered. After noting that "those values on which our success depends" are old and true, the source of progress throughout our history, the new president said he believed what's needed is a return to those truths. What is required of us now is a new era of responsibility—a recognition, on the part of every American, that we have duties to ourselves, our nation and the world, duties that we... seize gladly, firm in the knowledge that there is nothing... so defining of our character as giving our all to a difficult task. This is the price and promise of citizenship. This is the source of our confidence.... This is the meaning of our liberty and our creed.... [68]

It sounds pretty good. Yet as we reread the President's words now, in light of his actions during two years since, it is clear that responsibility and duty, citizenship and liberty, have a very different meaning in Mr. Obama's vocabulary from what they mean in yours and mine. He has misappropriated the language of *personal responsibility, freely chosen*, to cloak a radical agenda of *collective constraints, coercively imposed.*

Even so, this is the right conversation for Americans to be having with each other right now. Let the responsibility era begin, say I. There could not be a better frame for the policy debates and choices now before us.

DECADE OF DECISION

As important as politics are, let's remember what really gives definition to an era in American life. Ultimately it's not presidents and politicians, policies and programs. It is we the people, by how we think and how we act, that summon the spirit and set the course. Renewal of the responsibility ethic, already well begun in decades past, can advance in the coming decade regardless of who's in office, if *we* dedicate ourselves to that renewal.

In part this will certainly be a matter of what government does. But much of it must occur outside the political arena. The White House and Congress and the courts, the parties and universities and media, may at different times be with us or against us or indifferent. In the short term our concerns may sway them or may not. Longer term, institutions in this most open and idealistic of societies will not fail to reflect the convictions of an aroused citizenry.

What then should citizens be aroused about? The answer begins from the place where we find ourselves. An unsettled mood grips Americans right now. The country is economically distressed and war-weary on the one hand, ambivalent about its cool young leader on the other hand. There's an inclination to doubt the way things have been and to try new ideas on for size.

Old-fashioned responsibility could easily lose favor in this climate. The downtrend that Tytler described, apathy leading to dependence and then to bondage, could accelerate. The decadence that Glubb saw overtaking great nations after a couple of centuries, but which we fought off since the 1970s—"pessimism, materialism, frivolity, an influx of foreigners, the welfare state, and the weakening of religion… love of money, and the loss of a sense of duty"—might now finish us after all.[69]

This fatal aging of civilizations, aborting responsibility's rebirth, is still what the remnant has to resist. It's true that for the United States of America, constituted as we are, every decade is in some degree a decade of decision. But I believe the stakes are truly momentous at present. Great opportunities exist in the resilience, generosity, and creativity of our people and our system. Yet all could be lost if we don't strenuously counteract the dependence and decadence of which history warns.

"Some assembly required" says the packaging on each person's life here in the land of the free. A decade from now, Barack Obama and most of the other prominent names in the news will have been replaced by a new cast. The tone and direction of the United States by the year 2020 will be our doing, all of us together as citizens, more than the work of famous leaders or a powerful few. Personalities may change, but principles never do.

NO SUCCESS WITHOUT RESPONSIBILITY

One of the most fundamental principles is *No success without responsibility*. Our fidelity to it in the years ahead will determine whether the

United States thrives or falters. Let's come together on a responsibility agenda with ten priorities for the next ten years.

In civil society, responsible America must:

1. Strengthen families
2. Insist on learning
3. Renew a common culture
4. Expand charity
5. Expect more of churches

In the political arena, responsible America must:

6. Assert civic ownership
7. Rebuild our defenses
8. Resist over-government
9. Guard US sovereignty
10. Protect freedom of conscience

These are not the kind of goals where you have statistics or dates for an end point to say, "There, that's done." Nor could we, if I were Senate President again, put all this in a legislative package, pass everything, and call it good. These are basic attitudes and approaches for citizenship in the next American century.

Although headway has been made on most of them since the 1970s, the work is never done. Prioritizing these ten items with a horizon of 2020 can be an important down payment on the kind of country we want our children to inherit. Let's look at each of the ten in more detail:

1. STRENGTHEN FAMILIES

A free, responsible, and virtuous society rests on the marriage bond between men and women and the lifelong relationship of loyalty and caring between parents and children. Strengthening the family is the best way of limiting the irresponsibility and neediness that lead to excessive government.

Divorce damages everyone involved. So does illegitimacy. So does abortion. Social-science findings are conclusive on this. Controversy will continue over the response in public policy. This need not prevent us from working individually for stronger *traditional* families.

Adoption, single parenting, and same-sex households will be a widespread reality in the next American century. This cannot change the larger reality that the optimum for human flourishing is one man and one woman, married for life, procreating the next generation and raising them lovingly.

To repeat, this agenda for responsible America is about attitudes. A pro-family, pro-marriage, pro-life attitude is paramount.

2. INSIST ON LEARNING

Moral and intellectual ignorance is perhaps the worst form of irresponsibility, since it sets up all the others. The individual who has not been pushed to learn and helped to learn is left at the mercy of impulses from within and impositions from without. He careens through life like a car at night without steering, lights, or brakes. So an attitude that values learning, and that insists children must learn, is vital if we are to sustain responsible America.

Unless this fundamental change in thinking spreads from the bottom up, nothing will come (as nothing has come in the past) from talk of "education reform" and "better schools." Parents are the primary educators of the child. Academics and character cannot be separated. School and state *should* be separated, a goal that won't occur quickly, but toward which steps can begin now.

Charters, vouchers, tax credits, and home schooling should be encouraged. Competition, choice, and markets will deliver better learning performance at less cost than monopoly, bureaucracy, and unionism. Unions belong on assembly lines (if anywhere), not in classrooms.

The NEA and other teacher unions must be exposed as a money racket, a leftist indoctrination machine, and a Democratic Party auxiliary, unresponsive to their members and unconcerned with learning.

Ditto for the AAUP faculty union as a negative force at our universities, for the inflationary and learning-averse effects of taxpayer billions subsidizing higher education, and for the institutionalized irresponsibility of the US Department of Education propping up the whole P-20 system, preschool through grad school.

3. RENEW A COMMON CULTURE

Even if education begins to improve through our insistence on learning, irresponsibility will worsen unless the overall atmosphere of American life improves as well. Earlier in the book, exploring the convictions that define responsible America, we dwelt on the Declaration of Independence. Its principal author, Thomas Jefferson, called the Declaration "an expression of the American mind.[70] Who and what expresses the American mind today? How does the national conversation take place? Are we satisfied with that conversation? I'm not and I hope you're not.

Personal responsibility, an ethic of mutual obligation, a grateful recognition that life is a gift—these attitudes are little honored or

modeled in the cultural arena of our times. Our country's rebirth of responsibility since the 1970s has unfortunately made little or no headway in renewing the culture. Selfishness and coarseness pervade much of what we receive through the news media, movies and television, books and music, advertising and art. Celebrity saturates everything.

Jefferson: What is the American mind?

Renewing a common culture involves both quality and quantity. The idea marketplace, thankfully free and unfettered, responds to consumer demand. We can begin demanding from them the attributes of *what is best:* truth, beauty, goodness, integrity, faith, excellence, decency, duty, dignity, sacrifice, trust, unselfishness, reverence, and so on.

In that idea-marketplace, diverse as it is, we can also insist that American culture is *one*. English binds us together; it is the language of our shared future as well as our heritage. While the many cultural streams flowing together into this "first universal nation" are to be celebrated, the "ism" of multicultural propaganda is divisive and demoralizing to the land we love.[71] It should be politely but firmly rejected.

4. EXPAND CHARITY

Voluntary assistance to others in need, along with philanthropic giving for community benefit, meets the universal instinct of human decency as expressed in the Golden Rule and in Hillel's reflection, "If I am not for myself, then who will be for me? And if I am only for myself, then what am I?"[72]

Charity is also an important bulwark against excessive government and welfarism. Coercive redistribution is less tempting when unforced generosity prevails. Americans already lead the world in charitable good works, donating far more of their income and volunteering far more of their time than people in other nations (even at lower socio-economic levels) as Arthur Brooks has documented in his book, *Who Really Cares?* (New York, 2006). That's the good news.

The bad news is that despite welfare reform in the 1990s, tax-funded bureaucratic provision for more and more people's living standards continues to grow. The ethic of self-chosen benevolence to our neighbors must become stronger still. Otherwise we're headed for an absurd and socially corrosive situation where the law holds everyone "responsible" for everyone else's well-being and no one is responsible for himself.

While this sounds like something from *Alice in Wonderland* by Lewis Carroll, its real-world occurrence was noted by Carroll's contemporary, the French parliamentarian Frederic Bastiat, who wrote: "The state is the great fiction by which everybody seeks to live at the expense of everybody else."[73] That was in the 19th century. In our century, Bastiat's fiction is even more seductive, because the allure of statism is far stronger today, and our ingrained fidelity to responsibility ethic is far weaker. Led on by such notions as "duties to ourselves," the lofty psycho-babble from Obama's inaugural, we could end up collectivizing responsibility to the point where its free and personal dimension is lost.

Regardless of whether or not that is the President's intention with those words (and unfortunately I believe it was), our intention must be to expand charity for responsible America's sake.

5. EXPECT MORE OF CHURCHES

Weakening of religion is identified by Sir John Glubb as one of the terminal symptoms of decadence in *The Fate of Empires*. The United States, far more devout than any other major country in the world, might be thought to have no concerns on this score. Yet the concern is present and real. Collectivists seeking an omnipotent state and a sheeplike population, the future that Tocqueville feared, manipulate such ideas as responsibility, duty, progress, destiny, and even liberty, to achieve benign control over the whole people.

Was this Barack Obama's real intent in the inaugural passage quoted above? It seems so, more and more. The best defense against such entrapment is the Christian precept of "Render to Caesar, render to God," and the Jewish commandment against idolatry. "Put not your trust in princes," warns the Psalmist.[74]

Those truths don't ring from the pulpit, however. Religious bodies in America today—active, prosperous, and to all appearances free— too often drift with the materialist and collectivist undercurrent, neglecting the spiritual formation of their members. If the church won't shepherd its own flock, Caesar is quite ready to do so.

Praying people that we are, Americans remain uncomfortable with the question of whether humans can be good without God. Most of the evidence suggests we can't. I believe the only options are *personal* responsibility, the real thing, freely chosen in the fear of the Lord, or *purchased* responsibility, the counterfeit, imposed by legal compulsion and material allurements. Which will it be?

Our nation's greatness was forged when all of the responsibilities discussed in this agenda so far—family, learning, culture, and charity—were far less tied to government than is now the case, and far more shaped by the churches, both as to instruction and implementation. Recovering that balance won't be easy amidst the selfish and secular spirit of the age. But unless it is recovered, responsible America is at risk.

6. ASSERT CIVIC OWNERSHIP

Our responsibility agenda for the decade to 2020 is not primarily a political project. It is about living well as individuals in community. To live well, as we established at the outset of the book, is to live responsibly, to be ever mindful that life and the people we share it with are a gift, for which we owe a debt of gratitude. Politics enter in because law and government are needful to us as social beings, intelligent but imperfect, above the beasts and below the angels.

Politics will go better in the coming years if Americans begin to demand less of government by taking more responsibility for ourselves and our neighbors in the five areas considered above. But there is also a need for each citizen to "own" his place in the body politic responsibly and conscientiously, much as we own our physical bodies, homes, and other property. The reasoning goes this way: "This thing is partly mine, and I in turn am part of it. I'm at risk if it breaks down. As long as I live here, this thing and I can't disengage. So I need to actively *engage*, both for self-protection and to do my part."

Economists describe a problem called the tragedy of the commons, where land belonging to the public suffers abuse and neglect in contrast to the care given private lands. What everyone owns, no one owns, the rule seems to be. Our institutions of self-government are vulnerable in exactly this way. Each of us as citizens must take an *ownership attitude* as an antidote.

Economists again talk of an opposite attitude, rational ignorance, which is the shrug someone gives when he decides the cost of finding out exceeds the benefit of knowing. "In the long run we're all dead," some say when warned of the long-run dangers of deficits and debt, huge entitlements and weak defenses. Wrong; I don't want that kind of irresponsibility on my conscience. Responsibility has no expiration date. We must assert civic ownership; accept it; practice it.

7. REBUILD OUR DEFENSES

The idea that government's first job is to protect us against violent predators at home and abroad is so obvious that it should not need mentioning. Yet it's constantly forgotten. Man is a hopeful and gullible creature—a slow learner, as we've said—and Americans in particular have a pacific temperament.

There is no more dramatic example of responsibility's rebirth in our time, than the comeback of a morally and militarily disarmed United States from the late 1970s to emerge as the Cold War victor and the world's only superpower by the end of the 1980s. Now it seems the whole cycle may repeat. Feeling drained by the struggle since 2001 against a new kind of enemy in jihadist Islam and its state sponsors— a struggle that has gone remarkably well overall—the country voted in 2008 for leaders who say there is an easier way. It voted mostly on domestic issues in 2010. Specifically as to Iraq, Afghanistan, and Al Qaeda, the results will now play out.

These two elections did not change the realities of national survival, however. We know this is a dangerous world. We know America needs defending because she is a target of the envious, the ambitious, the fanatical, and the tyrannical. We know America is *worth* defending because she is good. So we are determined that America must have a defense second to none.

Russia is an aggressive threat. China is an aggressive threat. Iran, North Korea, Venezuela, Cuba, Hezbollah, and Hamas are their pawns. Jihadist Islam is an existential threat, if not by a doomsday attack then by the pressure of demography and the imposition of *dhimmitude* (a humiliating status of second-class citizenship for unbelievers). Apathy to dependence to bondage, the last act of the drama according to Tytler, can unfold through internal collapse or external conquest, with or without bloodshed. Facing those scenarios is unpleasant, but rational ignorance is no excuse.

Churchillian voices of warning are needed. When Winston Churchill and Franklin Roosevelt saved the world, the United States spent 40% of GDP on defense. We spent 9% under President Kennedy and 6% under President Reagan. Today, as a far wealthier nation than we were then—recession or not—we are spending only 4.6% of GDP on defense. The remnant should demand a significantly increased percentage in this decade of decision. We should demand an effective missile defense, which this country does not have. Our Chinese and Russian adversaries never sleep. Will we wake up in time?

8. RESIST OVER-GOVERNMENT

An America with backbone, America as it was meant to be, is an America with limited, constitutional government where most of life is about making our own choices (freedom) and taking the consequences (responsibility). That's far from the situation today. Responsibility's rebirth in this generation, notable as it was, witnessed only the slowing—not the reversal—of government growth in the Reagan and Clinton years. Irresponsible acceleration of government growth resumed in George W. Bush's time under a Republican Congress and White House. The acceleration dramatically worsened under the Democratic Congress and White House with Barack Obama in charge.[75]

Does government expand because of its own power dynamic, or because lapses of responsibility in civil society leave a vacuum?

Yes—both. There's a vicious circle. The moral entropy noted by Solzhenitsyn, Glubb, Tytler, and many other scholars weakens individuals and institutions. Unmet needs along with the state's inherent expansionism draw a political response. Civil society experiences some relief but suffers a further loss of vitality, and the spiral continues. With the atmosphere of economic crisis, it has intensified since 2008.

The only trouble with over-government is that it has never worked, never been able to deliver on its promises, and never will. The utterly predictable course of the past decade was foretold by Rudyard Kipling a century ago. "In the Carboniferous Epoch," he writes, mocking the ancient but ever-recurring fallacy,

> . . . we were promised abundance for all,
> By robbing selected Peter to pay for collective Paul;
> But, though we had plenty of money, there was nothing our money
>   could buy,
> And the Gods of the Copybook Headings said: *"If you don't work
>   you die."*[76]

Simple, as Reagan often said; not easy but simple. Something for nothing doesn't work. Command and control doesn't work. What sounds too good to be true usually is. Since this is an attitude agenda, not a campaign platform or a policy handbook, I will not discuss the dozens of issues in detail. One time-tested approach addresses them all. Defend free responsibility, responsible freedom, and resist over-government.

You know it when you see it: government health care, government energy policy, government climate regulations, government entitlements, government bailouts, government banks, government automakers, government handouts, government favoritism to unions, government tariffs, government muzzling of broadcasters, government deficits, government economic stimulus, government judges rewriting the constitution. Each without exception is a cure worse than the disease. Resist them.

I anticipate some will object that the grave problem of runaway government deserves more attention than I have given it with this lone item on an agenda of ten, this single brief section in the whole book. They will say that Caesar is the greatest threat to responsible America. The threat is serious indeed, I will agree. But the greatest threat is the person you see in the mirror. The next greatest is the person living next door to you. When hedged in by the other nine points of our responsibility agenda and confronted by the self-examining ethos I have urged throughout the book, over-government can be curbed. There is no stopping it otherwise. The line between good and evil runs right down the middle of every human heart, said Solzhenitsyn.[77] We get the government we deserve.

9. GUARD U.S. SOVEREIGNTY

We the American people became the world's freest, richest, most humane country by governing *ourselves* through consent and the rule of law to secure our God-given rights. We assumed our "separate and equal station among the powers of the earth" in 1776 and have held it since. But if current trends continue, all this will be submerged into global governance by the United Nations, the International Criminal Court, a proposed North American Union, and other worldwide or regional entities. "We are the world," that TV ad of a few years ago, was bad enough as a way to sell Coke. It is horrendous as a blueprint for US relations with nations of every description, democratic and despotic, law-abiding and brutal alike.

Transnational progressives, sincerely convinced that the nation-state is obsolete and a world polity is preferable, pursue their objectives from influential high-level positions in government, universities, foundations, and the media, out of public view. As we saw from the Bush administration's stealthy Security and Prosperity Partnership undertaking with Canada and Mexico, Republicans and Democrats alike are susceptible to the utopian visions of these "tranzies" and their profit-fixated corporate partners.

The latter, in unholy alliance with Democratic voting strategists and the guilty-America lobby, have also worked for open borders as 20 million illegal aliens poured into the country. Amnesty and a path to citizenship for these millions, which was defeated by a grassroots uprising in 2007, is again being pressed by Obama. Unequivocal sovereignty for the United States of America under our Constitution, including secure borders, is nonnegotiable for the continuance of our way of life. Accept no substitutes.

10. PROTECT FREEDOM OF CONSCIENCE

"I have sworn upon the altar of Almighty God, eternal hostility against every form of tyranny over the mind of man."[78] On the Jefferson Memorial in Washington, DC, above his statue, these words of the Virginian are inscribed. Each person must be at liberty to determine in his own heart right from wrong, good from evil, truth from falsehood. Actions that injure others can then certainly be punished, but laws purporting to forbid certain ideas and words are tyrannous and un-American—unacceptable. If angry minorities can persuade well-meaning majorities to invade personal conscience, Orwell's *1984* has come at last and we are no better than robots.

This threat is not speculative, it is here. Canada has tried journalists for criticizing Islam and clergymen for preaching against homosexuality. A member of the Dutch Parliament was put on trial for his condemnation of Muslim extremism. This kind of thought control is already being advocated in the United States in the form of speech codes, laws about hate crimes, and "human rights" commissions. Gays and Muslims, for all their antipathy to each other, join in pushing for it. Religious practice will be the first casualty. Scholarship, the press, and political expression are also endangered as law decrees what we may not say about taboo subjects from abortion clinics to candidates for office. Holocaust denial has been criminalized in Europe, and by analogy there is now a social stigma on "global warming denial."

Where will it stop? Zealotry even trumps the First Amendment, in Sen. John McCain's view. "So-called free speech" must yield to clean government, he has said. Victimhood seems to trump the ideals of Jefferson and Voltaire in the view of President Obama, who played the race card shamelessly in his run for the White House. Moral accountability, the true meaning of responsibility, is destroyed if the mind and conscience of individuals are forced into a mold by governmental coercion or its insidious proxy, political correctness. This danger will intensify in the coming decade. We must not yield.

OUR ACTIONS MATTER

The United States does not lack for threats and problems right now. Talk of new opportunities may sound ironic as we look at one challenge after another in this responsibility agenda for the year 2020. Yet turning difficulty into opportunity has been the story of our country for four centuries past. This next American century holds more of the same.

The present difficulties could bring out the best in responsible America. Or the situation may fool us and frighten us into bad decisions that bring back the responsibility deficit. A generation of remarkable gains could be undone. That's why I call these Obama years and their sequel a decade of decision. Things could go either way.

Our agenda in civil society should be to strengthen families, insist on learning, renew a common culture, expand charity, and expect more of churches. In the political arena, building on this foundation, our agenda should be to assert civic ownership, rebuild our defenses, resist over-government, guard US sovereignty, and protect freedom of conscience.

Enemies abroad and irresponsibility at home darken the outlook, but they are not the worst threat we face. The undertow of weariness and carelessness is worse. Lincoln led magnificently in wartime. But long before the Union was broken and saved, he warned of a far future when "the silent armies of time" might bloodlessly take America down—simply through our forgetting who and what we are.[79] Has that future come? Not if you and I can help it.

It's true what Barack Obama said upon taking the oath of office. We do need "a new era of responsibility—a recognition, on the part of every American, that we have duties to ourselves, our nation and the world." But the President's words are only words until actions make them real.

Our actions will matter more than his—which is good, because such rhetoric as "duties to ourselves" could mean anything or nothing. It could become a pretext for utopian irresponsibility, when combined with other ambiguous but ambitious ideas from the same speech— such as "remaking America" and "God calls on us to shape an uncertain destiny."[80]

All the more reason why we of the remnant, Element R, need our own clear plan, no matter what Mr. Obama's may be. Our responsibility agenda of ten goals can be that plan.

CHAPTER 14

WHERE IT STARTS

Colossians 3:23

Been to any funerals lately? I'm at the age when you start going to more of them. When paying last respects, I am always reminded that the number of mourners who come to the graveside for any of us will ultimately depend more on the weather that day, than on what an important person one thinks himself to be.

It's a big world, and it moves on. A very few words will sum up the remembrance of you or me when we're gone. By anticipating what we'd like others to say then, we begin to live more fully now. A title of honor to which any citizen might keenly aspire is *Responsible American.*

How fine to have this as a reputation in our lifetimes or a tribute from posterity—to have one's name connected with the name of our beloved country and the accolade, "Well done." You'd never make a bumper sticker of it, of course; what irresponsibility. Modestly is the only way it could be undertaken; a thing to be worn lightly and lived quietly, never spoken of.

The banter of a talk show host and his callers, lauding each other as "great Americans," is similar but not as deep as this. This is bone deep, good and true. It's exactly opposite to those "ugly Americans" of whom a noted book was written years ago and to whom the left in this country still charges all sorts of wrongs.[81]

The alleged wrongs are in many instances invented and, for the rest, exaggerated. But the ugliness of irresponsible citizens is real enough across the social and political spectrum. Responsible Americans, citizens dedicated to the responsibility ethic and alert to the responsibility deficit, are needed as urgently today as they were in 1775 and 1975.

THE RESPONSIBLE AMERICAN

To understand personal responsibility, mutual obligation, and the life of gratitude is to understand how each of us, in smaller or larger ways, is not only shaped by our times but helps shape them. There is a lot of power and potential in knowing that. There is also a feeling of weight on your shoulders, satisfying but serious. This is for keeps; it's not a drill. Our decisions matter. Others are counting on us.

With emphasis on the chance to help shape our times, and the price of failing to do so, this book is presented as a Citizen's Guide. The objective is not just information. It is motivation. The reader is urged to ask himself: What can I do? What can I be? What can I give? Where shall I aim?

Even when our discussion has been on a grand scale—civilizations, cycles, centuries, the sweep of American history, responsibility in the mind of the Founders, the remnant and Element R—individuals were at the center. Persons struggling to choose right from wrong, one at a time, made all of it happen.

Every choice mattered, even when the person hoped or feared it wouldn't. No one so obscure that someone else didn't feel a tie. No deed so secret that conscience didn't see. Hence the responsible American, the individual with the future in his hands.

Hence *personal* responsibility. The individualizing adjective has never been more important than today. Honest or purposeful confusion about things like duty and obligation is a very real danger in our country right now.

We noted in the previous chapter Barack Obama's deceptively appealing inaugural rhetoric about "a new era of responsibility." The sinister undertone emerged a week later when he gave another speech warning that responsibility is incompatible with businesses seeking "to make profits."

The tone of this president's new era has since become all too clear. We have entered a time when citizens are being told responsibility requires us to accept the nationalizing of industries, the reduction of living standards for climate's sake, the surrender of U.S. sovereignty, or the suppression of our religious beliefs.

TEN WORDS

What an insult. Redefining responsibility to mean capitulation to the collective is an irresponsible lie. Responsibility can only mean individual integrity: "If it is to be, it is up to me."

In terms of human potential, those ten little words of two letters each are perhaps the most powerful sentence in the English language. So said an aged black pastor to a student audience when I was director of seminars at Hillsdale College back in the '80s.

Often fearing for his life as a civil-rights worker in the segregated South of the 1950s, the old man recalled, what brought him through, time and again, was not only his deep faith but also the can-do, must-do impulse of this responsible American's credo.

That day changed my life. An already earnest attitude of self-responsibility was redoubled in me, and it has remained so. The uneven report card I have earned through the years in living this out, as examined earlier, does not lessen my gratitude for the insight. In some ways those ten words have been the making of me as a citizen.

Dr. King's legacy lives on

What is your American credo? What life-lessons have you learned that might be worth sharing with others as Dr. King's battle-scarred disciple did? What have you contributed as a citizen? What more do you aspire to contribute? Stirring you to think about these questions has been my whole purpose here.

With the convictions I set down in Part One, the life lessons related and graded in Part Two, and the responsibilities we've looked at in Part Three, the idea was to open a discussion. I've made a start on my answers to the questions. But your answers have to be *yours*. Are they coming into focus?

"If it is to be, it is up to me."

APPENDIX

BACKGROUND FOR THE PREFACE

AMERICA THE BEAUTIFUL

Words by Katharine Lee Bates
Melody by Samuel Ward

(1) O beautiful for spacious skies,
  For amber waves of grain,
  For purple mountain majesties
  Above the fruited plain!
  America! America!
  God shed his grace on thee
  And crown thy good with
    brotherhood
  From sea to shining sea!

(2) O beautiful for pilgrim feet
  Whose stern impassioned stress
  A thoroughfare of freedom beat
  Across the wilderness!
  America! America!
  God mend thine every flaw,
  Confirm thy soul in self-control,
  Thy liberty in law!

(3) O beautiful for heroes proved
  In liberating strife.
  Who more than self their country
    loved
  And mercy more than life!
  America! America!
  May God thy gold refine
  Till all success be nobleness
  And every gain divine!

(4) O beautiful for patriot dream
  That sees beyond the years
  Thine alabaster cities gleam
  Undimmed by human tears!
  America! America!
  God shed his grace on thee
  And crown thy good with
    brotherhood
  From sea to shining sea!

(5) O beautiful for halcyon skies,
  For amber waves of grain,
  For purple mountain majesties
  Above the enameled plain!
  America! America!
  God shed his grace on thee
  Till souls wax fair as earth and air
  And music-hearted sea!

(6) O beautiful for pilgrim feet,
  Whose stem impassioned stress
  A thoroughfare for freedom beat
  Across the wilderness!
  America! America!
  God shed his grace on thee
  Till paths be wrought through
    wilds of thought
  By pilgrim foot and knee!

(7) O beautiful for glory-tale
Of liberating strife
When once and twice,
for man's avail
Men lavished precious life!
America! America!
God shed his grace on thee
Till selfish gain no longer stain
The banner of the free!

(8) O beautiful for patriot dream
That sees beyond the years
Thine alabaster cities gleam
Undimmed by human tears!
America! America!
God shed his grace on thee
Till nobler men keep once again
Thy whiter jubilee!

BACKGROUND FOR CHAPTER 3:

EDITORIAL CREDO OF *ANDREWS' AMERICA*

Every month from August 1994 to January 2007, I produced *Andrews' America*, a one-page journal of "notes on our times," and sent it via postal mail and email to several hundred friends across the country. The April 1995 issue contained this outline of personal convictions, which I called "our editorial credo in a dozen bites." I stand by this credo today, except that as explained in Chapter 3, I would now restate the fourth point to say: "Freedom and its obverse, responsibility, are the master values for ordering human life."

1. We live in a God-governed universe, not a vast random accident.
2. Truth exists, and is knowable by you and me.
3. Morality is built into the very structure of reality.
4. Freedom is the master value.
5. Rights come from the Creator not the state, and they inhere in individuals not groups.
6. Free markets and private property best allocate resources and multiply wealth.
7. Democracy is possible because we are not beasts, and necessary because we are not angels.
8. The few can never know enough or care enough to rightly rule the many.
9. A word is worth a thousand pictures.

10. Newer is not necessarily better.

11. You cannot criticize the Bible; it criticizes you.

12. People matter most of all.

BACKGROUND FOR CHAPTER 3:

THE DECLARATION OF INDEPENDENCE

IN CONGRESS, July 4, 1776.

The unanimous Declaration of the thirteen united States of America,

When in the Course of human events, it becomes necessary for one people to dissolve the political bands which have connected them with another, and to assume among the powers of the earth, the separate and equal station to which the Laws of Nature and of Nature's God entitle them, a decent respect to the opinions of mankind requires that they should declare the causes which impel them to the separation.

We hold these truths to be self-evident, that all men are created equal, that they are endowed by their Creator with certain unalienable Rights, that among these are Life, Liberty and the pursuit of Happiness.—That to secure these rights, Governments are instituted among Men, deriving their just powers from the consent of the governed, — That whenever any Form of Government becomes destructive of these ends, it is the Right of the People to alter or to abolish it, and to institute new Government, laying its foundation on such principles and organizing its powers in such form, as to them shall seem most likely to effect their Safety and Happiness. Prudence, indeed, will dictate that Governments long established should not be changed for light and transient causes; and accordingly all experience hath shewn, that mankind are more disposed to suffer, while evils are sufferable, than to right themselves by abolishing the forms to which they are accustomed. But when a long train of abuses and usurpations, pursuing invariably the same Object evinces a design to reduce them under absolute Despotism, it is their right, it is their duty, to throw off such Government, and to provide new Guards for their future security.—Such has been the patient sufferance of these Colonies; and such is now the necessity which constrains them to alter their former Systems of Government. The history of the present King of Great Britain is a history of repeated injuries and usurpations, all having in direct object the establishment of an absolute Tyranny over these States. To prove this, let Facts be submitted to a candid world.

He has refused his Assent to Laws, the most wholesome and necessary for the public good.

He has forbidden his Governors to pass Laws of immediate and pressing importance, unless suspended in their operation till his Assent should be obtained; and when so suspended, he has utterly neglected to attend to them.

He has refused to pass other Laws for the accommodation of large districts of people, unless those people would relinquish the right of Representation in the Legislature, a right inestimable to them and formidable to tyrants only.

He has called together legislative bodies at places unusual, uncomfortable, and distant from the depository of their public Records, for the sole purpose of fatiguing them into compliance with his measures.

He has dissolved Representative Houses repeatedly, for opposing with manly firmness his invasions on the rights of the people.

He has refused for a long time, after such dissolutions, to cause others to be elected; whereby the Legislative powers, incapable of Annihilation, have returned to the People at large for their exercise; the State remaining in the mean time exposed to all the dangers of invasion from without, and convulsions within.

He has endeavoured to prevent the population of these States; for that purpose obstructing the Laws for Naturalization of Foreigners; refusing to pass others to encourage their migrations hither, and raising the conditions of new Appropriations of Lands.

He has obstructed the Administration of Justice, by refusing his Assent to Laws for establishing Judiciary powers.

He has made Judges dependent on his Will alone, for the tenure of their offices, and the amount and payment of their salaries.

He has erected a multitude of New Offices, and sent hither swarms of Officers to harrass our people, and eat out their substance.

He has kept among us, in times of peace, Standing Armies without the Consent of our legislatures.

He has affected to render the Military independent of and superior to the Civil power.

He has combined with others to subject us to a jurisdiction foreign to our constitution, and unacknowledged by our laws; giving his Assent to their Acts of pretended Legislation:

For Quartering large bodies of armed troops among us:

For protecting them, by a mock Trial, from punishment for any Murders which they should commit on the Inhabitants of these States:

For cutting off our Trade with all parts of the world:

For imposing Taxes on us without our Consent:

For depriving us in many cases, of the benefits of Trial by Jury:

For transporting us beyond Seas to be tried for pretended offences

For abolishing the free System of English Laws in a neighbouring Province, establishing therein an Arbitrary government, and enlarging its Boundaries so as to render it at once an example and fit instrument for introducing the same absolute rule into these Colonies:

For taking away our Charters, abolishing our most valuable Laws, and altering fundamentally the Forms of our Governments:

For suspending our own Legislatures, and declaring themselves invested with power to legislate for us in all cases whatsoever.

He has abdicated Government here, by declaring us out of his Protection and waging War against us.

He has plundered our seas, ravaged our Coasts, burnt our towns, and destroyed the lives of our people.

He is at this time transporting large Armies of foreign Mercenaries to compleat the works of death, desolation and tyranny, already begun with circumstances of Cruelty & perfidy scarcely parallelled in the most barbarous ages, and totally unworthy the Head of a civilized nation.

He has constrained our fellow Citizens taken Captive on the high Seas to bear Arms against their Country, to become the executioners of their friends and Brethren, or to fall themselves by their Hands.

He has excited domestic insurrections amongst us, and has endeavoured to bring on the inhabitants of our frontiers, the merciless Indian Savages, whose known rule of warfare, is an undistinguished destruction of all ages, sexes and conditions.

In every stage of these Oppressions We have Petitioned for Redress in the most humble terms: Our repeated Petitions have been answered only by repeated injury. A Prince whose character is thus marked by every act which may define a Tyrant, is unfit to be the ruler of a free people.

Nor have We been wanting in attentions to our Brittish brethren. We have warned them from time to time of attempts by their legislature to extend an unwarrantable jurisdiction over us. We have reminded them of the circumstances of our emigration and settlement here. We have appealed to their native justice and magnanimity, and we have conjured them by the ties of our common kindred to disavow these usurpations, which, would inevitably interrupt our connections and correspondence. They too have been deaf to the voice of justice and of consanguinity. We must, therefore, acquiesce in the necessity, which denounces our Separation, and hold them, as we hold the rest of mankind, Enemies in War, in Peace Friends.

We, therefore, the Representatives of the united States of America, in General Congress, Assembled, appealing to the Supreme Judge of the world for the rectitude of our intentions, do, in the Name, and by Authority of the good People of these Colonies, solemnly publish and declare, That these United Colonies are, and of Right ought to be Free and Independent States; that they are Absolved from all Allegiance to the British Crown, and that all political connection between them and the State of Great Britain, is and ought to be totally dissolved; and that as Free and Independent States, they have full Power to levy War, conclude Peace, contract Alliances, establish Commerce, and to do all other Acts and Things which Independent States may of right do. And for the support of this Declaration, with a firm reliance on the protection of divine Providence, we mutually pledge to each other our Lives, our Fortunes and our sacred Honor.

Source: http://www.archives.gov/exhibits/charters/declaration_transcript.html

BACKGROUND FOR CHAPTER 12:
THE GODS OF THE COPYBOOK HEADINGS
By Rudyard Kipling

As I pass through my incarnations in every age and race,
I make my proper prostrations to the Gods of the Market Place.
Peering through reverent fingers I watch them flourish and fall,
And the Gods of the Copybook Headings, I notice, outlast them all.

We were living in trees when they met us. They showed us each in
    turn
That Water would certainly wet us, as Fire would certainly burn:
But we found them lacking in Uplift, Vision and Breadth of Mind,
So we left them to teach the Gorillas while we followed the March of
    Mankind.

We moved as the Spirit listed. They never altered their pace,
Being neither cloud nor wind-borne like the Gods of the Market
    Place,
But they always caught up with our progress, and presently word
    would come
That a tribe had been wiped off its icefield, or the lights had gone out
    in Rome.

With the Hopes that our World is built on they were utterly out of
    touch,
They denied that the Moon was Stilton; they denied she was even
    Dutch;
They denied that Wishes were Horses; they denied that a Pig had
    Wings;
So we worshipped the Gods of the Market Who promised these
    beautiful things.

When the Cambrian measures were forming, They promised
    perpetual peace.
They swore, if we gave them our weapons, that the wars of the tribes
    would cease.
But when we disarmed They sold us and delivered us bound to our
    foe,
And the Gods of the Copybook Headings said: "Stick to the Devil
    you know."

On the first Feminian Sandstones we were promised the Fuller Life
(Which started by loving our neighbour and ended by loving his
    wife)
Till our women had no more children and the men lost reason and
    faith,
And the Gods of the Copybook Headings said: "The Wages of Sin is
    Death."

In the Carboniferous Epoch we were promised abundance for all,
By robbing selected Peter to pay for collective Paul;
But, though we had plenty of money, there was nothing our money
    could buy,
And the Gods of the Copybook Headings said: "If you don't work
    you die."

Then the Gods of the Market tumbled, and their smooth-tongued
   wizards withdrew
And the hearts of the meanest were humbled and began to believe it
   was true
That All is not Gold that Glitters, and Two and Two make Four
And the Gods of the Copybook Headings limped up to explain it
   once more.

As it will be in the future, it was at the birth of Man
There are only four things certain since Social Progress began.
That the Dog returns to his Vomit and the Sow returns to her Mire,
And the burnt Fool's bandaged finger goes wabbling back to the Fire;

And that after this is accomplished, and the brave new world begins
When all men are paid for existing and no man must pay for his sins,
As surely as Water will wet us, as surely as Fire will burn,
The Gods of the Copybook Headings with terror and slaughter
   return!

Source: http://www.kipling.org.uk/poems_copybook.htm

Books and Authors Cited or Mentioned

Adams, John. *The Works of John Adams,* edited by Charles Francis Adams (Boston: Little, Brown, 1854)

Allen, William B. *George Washington: America's First Progressive* (New York: Peter Lang, 2008)

Barone, Michael. *Hard America, Soft America: Competition vs. Coddling and the Battle for the Nation's Future* (New York, Three Rivers Press, 2004)

Bernstein, Carl, and Bob Woodward. *All the President's Men* (New York: Simon and Schuster, 1974)

Bolt, Robert *A Man for All Seasons,* (New York, Vintage International, 1990)

Boorstin, Daniel, Ed. *An American Primer* (Chicago: University of Chicago Press, 1966)

Bowen, Catherine Drinker. *Miracle at Philadelphia* (Boston: Atlantic-Little, Brown, 1966)

Brooks, Arthur C. *Who Really Cares?* (New York: Basic Books, 2006)

Burdick, Eugene, and William Lederer, *The Ugly American* (New York: Norton, 1958)

Friedman, Milton, and Rose Friedman. *Free to Choose: A Personal Statement* (San Diego: Harcourt Brace, 1990)

Glubb, Sir John. *The Fate of Empires and Search for Survival* (Edinburgh: William Blackwood, 1978)

Goldwater, Barry. *The Conscience of a* Conservative (Blacksburg VA: Wilder Publications, 2009)

Hayek, Friedrich A. *The Road to Serfdom* (Chicago: University of Chicago Press, 1944)

Hayward , Steven F. *The Index of Leading Environmental Indicators* (San Francisco: Pacific Research Institute, 2009)

Jaffa, Harry V. *Crisis of the House Divided: An Interpretation of the Issues in the Lincoln-Douglas Debates* (Chicago: University of Chicago Press, 1982)

Jaffa, Harry V. *A New Birth of Freedom: Abraham Lincoln and the Coming of the Civil War* (Lanham MD: Rowman & Littlefield, 2000)

Jefferson, Thomas. *The Writings of Thomas Jefferson,* edited by Andrew A. Lipscomb (Washington: Thomas Jefferson Memorial Association, 1907)

Krannawitter, Thomas. *An Introduction to Citizenship for New Americans* (Claremont CA: The Claremont Institute, 2002)

Krogh, Egil, and Matthew Krogh, *Integrity: Good People, Bad Choices, and Life Lessons from the White House* (New York: PublicAffairs, 2007).

Lewis, C. S. *Mere Christianity* (New York: Macmillan, 1960)

Lindskoog, Katherine, Ed. *Around the Year with C. S. Lewis and His Friends* (Norwalk CT: Gibson, 1986)

Madison, James; Alexander Hamilton; and John Jay. *The Federalist* edited by Jacob E. Cooke (Cleveland: Meridian Books, 1961)

Meadows, Donella H. *The Limits to Growth: A Report for the Club of Rome's Project on the Predicament of Mankind* (Washington: Potoma Associates, 1974)

Miller, Kevin. *Freedom Nationally, Virtue Locally—or Socialism* (Denver: Denali Press, 2010)

Moore, Stephen, and Julian L. Simon. *It's Getting Better All the Time: The Top 100 Trends of the Past 100 Years* (Washington: Cato Institute, 2001)

Muir, John. *John of the Mountains: The Unpublished Journals of John Muir,* edited by Linnie Marsh Wolfe (Madison: University of Wisconsin Press, 1979)

Murray, Charles. *Losing Ground: American Social Policy 1950-1980* (New York: Basic Books, 1984)

Nock, Albert Jay. *The State of the Union,* edited by Charles Hamilton (Indianapolis: Liberty Press, 1991)

Orwell, George. *1984* (London: Martin Secker, 1949)

Piereson, James. *Camelot and the Cultural Revolution* (New York: Encounter Books, 2007)

Smith, Adam. *An Inquiry into the Nature and Causes of the Wealth of Nations* (Oxford: Oxford University Press, 2008)

Smith, Adam. *The Theory of Moral Sentiments* (New York: Penguin Classics, 2010)

Solzhenitsyn, Alexander. *One Day in the Life of Ivan Denisovich* (New York: Bantam, 1963)

Solzhenitsyn, Alexander. "A World Split Apart" *National Review,* July 7, 1978

Solzhenitsyn, Alexander. *August 1914* (New York: Penguin Books, 1990)

Tocqueville, Alexis. *Democracy in America,* Reeve translation edited by Philips Bradley (New York: Knopf, 1945)

Wattenberg, Ben. *The First Universal Nation* (New York: Free Press, 1990)

White, Theodore H. *Breach of Faith: The Fall of Richard Nixon* (New York: Atheneum, 1975)

Will, George F. *Statecraft as Soulcraft* (New York: Simon and Schuster, 1984)

A Bibliophile's Note in Closing

"What ten books have impacted your life the most?" In response to this question from my friend Kevin Teasley, a leader in the school choice movement, I named the following titles in the November 2002 issue of *Andrews' America,* giving a reason for each:

- *Science and Health,* by Mary Baker Eddy, taught me to love the Bible.

- *The Bible* engaged me with Jesus Christ.

- *The Everlasting Man,* by G. K. Chesterton, grounded me in Christian tradition.

- *Mere Christianity,* by C. S. Lewis, showed me the beauty of truth.

- *The Conscience of a Conservative*, by Barry Goldwater, awakened me politically.

- *The Law*, by Frederic Bastiat, was my primer in political economy.

- *The Road to Serfdom*, by F. A. Hayek, set me against collectivism.

- *Ideas Have Consequences*, by Richard Weaver, bonded me to the permanent things.

- *The Lord of the Rings*, by J. R. R. Tolkien, convinced me that life is a sacred quest.

- *A Man for All Seasons*, by Robert Bolt, inspired me with the possibility of heroic integrity.

Today, nearly a decade later, I stand by the list. Readers will notice that it overlaps significantly with the foregoing bibliography.

1. Address to the New Jersey Senate, Feb. 21, 1861. See http://showcase.netins.net/web/creative/lincoln/speeches/trenton1.htm

2. See Appendix for the full text of lyrics to "America the Beautiful."

3. The Bible verses cited at the head of each chapter are more personal than public in their significance. These are golden texts for self-instruction that I had in mind, or should have had in mind, when living through the experiences discussed in a particular chapter. The exact phrasing that always resonates most deeply with me, as the reader will learn, is that of the King James Version.

4. Bill Clinton carried Colorado with a plurality in 1992.

5. Isaiah 6:8 (King James Version)

6. Thomas Krannawitter, *An Introduction to Citizenship for New Americans* (Claremont CA: The Claremont Institute, 2002), pp. 11-12

7. "Remnant" as a name for the unconquered faithful few is used many times by Isaiah, Jeremiah, Ezekiel, and other Old Testament prophets, and is echoed by the Apostle Paul, who quotes Isaiah 10:22 in Romans 9:27 (King James Version). Many conservatives cherish Albert Jay Nock's modern application of the remnant idea in his 1936 essay, "Isaiah's Job." See Charles Hamilton, ed., *The State of the Union* (Indianapolis: Liberty Press, 1991), p. 124.

8. On the day the Constitution was signed, Sept. 17, 1787, according to a letter from James Madison to Thomas Jefferson, Franklin told his fellow delegates that after months of uncertainty about the significance of a sun motif carved in the chair of the presiding officer, George Washington, "Now at length I have the happiness to know that it is a rising and not a setting sun." Quoted in Catherine Drinker Bowen, *Miracle at Philadelphia* (Boston: Atlantic-Little, Brown, 1966), p. 263.

9. Because of miseducation by the mass media and the schools, readers may stumble at the idea of "spectacular environmental gains." The data are conclusive, however, as spelled out in such books as *The Index of Leading Environmental Indicators* by Steven F. Hayward (San Francisco: Pacific Research Institute, 2009) and *It's Getting Better All the Time: The Top 100 Trends of the Past 100 Years* by Stephen Moore and Julian L. Simon (Washington: Cato Institute, 2001).

10. See Appendix for the full text of my *Andrews' America* editorial credo.

11. See Appendix for the full text of the Declaration of Independence.

12. The words of Jesus are from Matthew 5:14 (King James Version.) For the Winthrop quotation, see Daniel Boorstin, ed., *An American Primer*, Vol. 1 (Chicago: University of Chicago Press, 1966), p. 22. For one of Reagan's many uses of the phrase see his farewell address from the Oval Office, Jan. 11, 1989. http://www.americanrhetoric.com/speeches/ronaldreaganfarewelladdress.html

13. From the majority opinion by Justice Anthony Kennedy in *Planned Parenthood vs. Casey*, 1992, holding that in general a state may not legislate to prevent a mother from taking the life of her unborn child. See http://www.law.cornell.edu/supct/html/historics/USSC_CR_0505_0833_ZS.html

14. Reminiscence of A. C. Harwood, quoted in Katherine Lindskoog, Ed., *Around the Year with C. S. Lewis and His Friends* (Norwalk CT: Gibson, 1986) entry for Nov. 29.

15. William B. Allen, *George Washington: America's First Progressive* (New York: Peter Lang, 2008)

16. See http://www.nationalcenter.org/ReaganChoosing1964.html . The full quotation reads: "You and I are told increasingly that we have to choose between a left or right, but I would like to suggest that there is no such thing as a left or right. There is only an up or down—up to man's age-old dream, the ultimate in individual freedom consistent with law and order—or down to the ant heap of totalitarianism, and regardless of their sincerity, their humanitarian motives, those who would trade our freedom for security have embarked on this downward course."

17. Theodore H. White, *Breach of Faith: The Fall of Richard Nixon* (New York: Atheneum, 1975)

17. See Catherine Drinker Bowen, *Miracle at Philadelphia* (Boston: Atlantic-Little, Brown, 1966), p. 263

19. The famous passage is supposedly from a book by Alexander Tytler called *The Fall of the Athenian Republic*, but no such book has been verified. Nor does the passage appear in *Universal History*, Tytler's most comprehensive and definitive book.

20. Sir John Glubb, *The Fate of Empires and Search for Survival* (Edinburgh: William Blackwood, 1978), p. 28. I am indebted to former U.S. Senator Hank Brown for acquainting me with this valuable book.

21. *Ibid.*, p. 11

22. *Ibid.*, p. 13

23. *Ibid.*, p. 14

24. *Ibid.*, p. 27

25. *Ibid.*, pp. 29, 46

26. *Ibid.*, p. 29

27. *Ibid.*, p. 46

28. See Linnie Marsh Wolfe, Ed. *John of the Mountains: The Unpublished Journals of John Muir* (Madison: University of Wisconsin Press, 1979)

29. It was Charles H. Percy, Republican platform committee chairman in 1960 and later U.S. Senator from Illinois, who obtained my page appointment along with those of his twin daughters, Valerie and Sharon. Chuck Percy's generous encouragement to me, then and thereafter, glows in memory.

30. This was my first occasion to work personally with Bill Armstrong, then a congressman representing Colorado's 5th District, later a U.S. senator, and today the president of Colorado Christian University, where I currently work. The friendship and Christian example of Bill, his wife Ellen, and their son Wil have been a treasure to Donna and me for these many years.

31. As C. S. Lewis puts it in *Mere Christianity* (New York: Macmillan, 1960), p. 169, "…you cannot go on indefinitely being just an ordinary, decent egg. We must hatch or go bad."

32. See Robert Bolt, *A Man for All Seasons*, (New York, Vintage International, 1990) p. 140. The play had long been one of our readings in the freshman honors course on "Paradoxes of the Human Condition" at the Colorado School of Mines.

33. See George F. Will, *Statecraft as Soulcraft* (New York: Simon and Schuster, 1984). A recent book of related interest is *Freedom Nationally, Virtue Locally—or Socialism* (Denver: Denali Press, 2010), by Kevin Miller, my colleague at Centennial Institute. Miller doubts

the efficacy, and fears the perverse effects, of "virtue legislation" at almost any level of government, especially the federal level. I share his concern, up to a point—but I give more weight than he does to the moral and ethical formation effected in public consciousness by law's permissions and prohibitions. It remains a matter of friendly debate between us.

34. State senators are usually eligible for eight consecutive years of service, two full terms. But having served over half of Mike Coffman's unexpired term after 1998 (two years and two weeks, to be exact), I was constitutionally allowed only one full term of my own.

35. Here I paraphrase from the second president's famous letter of October 11, 1798, to officers of the Massachusetts Militia, quoted in Charles Francis Adams, Ed., *The Works of John Adams* (Boston: Little, Brown, 1854), p. 228. Adams's exact words were, "Our Constitution was made only for a moral and religious people. It is wholly inadequate to the government of any other."

36. Bud Krogh, as everyone called him, had been five years ahead of me at Principia in high school and college. Working under John Ehrlichman in 1969, he helped bring my name to Ron Ziegler's attention, which led to my being hired at the White House. No one who was convicted in the Watergate scandal has distilled the moral and ethical lessons of that era more thoughtfully than Bud has done in a book he co-authored with his son. See Egil Krogh and Matthew Krogh, *Integrity: Good People, Bad Choices, and Life Lessons from the White House* (New York: PublicAffairs, 2007).

37. The text mentions our family's spiritual pilgrimage only in passing, since it is peripheral to the purpose of this book—though of supreme importance to us personally. What occurred was that in the mid-1990s, after long consideration, my wife and I amicably resigned from the Christian Science church over irreconcilable issues of biblical interpretation. We now belong to a Presbyterian church, as do our three children. All of us are grateful for countless experiences of God's grace in our lives, from childhood to the present day.

38. Isaiah 6:8 (King James Version)

39. Gordon Lightfoot's whimsical ballad about Don Quixote (written in 1972 and later used as the title song of his eighth album in 1998) was nominated by John Fritschler, the Colorado State University student who was my driver during the campaign, as our theme song for the 1990 race. We about wore out the cassette tape on those long highway miles. "Reaching for his saddlebag, he takes a rusty sword into his hand," says one verse. "Then striking up a knightly pose, he shouts across the ocean to the shore, till he can shout no more." That was me: shouting for freedom and responsibility till I could shout no more. See http://www.gordonlightfoot.com/Lyrics/DQ.txt .

40. Extreme in all sorts of ways, was I—if you believed the opposition. "Why, John Andrews, you don't even like government," scolded Roy Romer in one debate, with the faux shock at which he excelled. That I could laugh off. But it stung much worse—and mortified our family and Christian Scientist friends—when the media opened fire on my belief in spiritual healing, based on support I had offered to Spindrift Inc., an Illinois nonprofit doing lab tests on the effects of prayer. "Andrews tied to experiments," headlined the *Grand Junction Daily Sentinel* on Sept. 23, 1990. "Organization studied power of prayer over mung beans." The Associated Press soon splashed the story nationally, further weakening my already anemic campaign. It was either a militant skeptics group, or my Democratic opponents, that researched and broke the story; I never found out for sure. But the political impact was deadly, despite my self-mockery at dinners for weeks afterward—"Before we start, I'd like to bless the salad bar"—and as long as I live, there will be some people in Colorado who think first of mung beans and weirdness when they hear my name.

41. Donna, to her everlasting credit, tried to warn me of this before it was too late. I rejected her counsel and resented it. Regrettably this husband's arrogance has had nine lives.

42. If this sounds like the misplaced focus on scalps that I just deplored, it isn't that. I am saying that greater and more enduring success in governance can paradoxically result from less attention to tactics and more focus on big ideas. As the maxim goes, take good care of the policy, and the politics will take care of themselves.

43. Proverbs 27:6 (King James Version)

44. Alexander Solzhenitsyn, "A World Split Apart," *National Review*, July 7, 1978, pp. 837-841

45. *Ibid.*, p. 837

46. *Ibid.*, pp. 840, 839

47. *Ibid.*, p. 838

48. *Ibid.*

49. *Ibid.*, p. 841

50. *Ibid.*, p. 838

51. *Ibid.*, p. 855

52. *Ibid.*, p. 841

53. Sir John Glubb, *The Fate of Empires and Search for Survival* (Edinburgh: William Blackwood, 1978), p. 46.

54. Alexander Solzhenitsyn, "A World Split Apart," *National Review*, July 7, 1978, p. 841

55. *Ibid.*

56. See http://teachingamericanhistory.org/library/index.asp?document=41

57. Alexander Solzhenitsyn, "A World Split Apart," *National Review*, July 7, 1978, p. 855

58. See http://www.nationalcenter.org/ReaganChoosing1964.html

59. See Appendix for the full text of "The Gods of the Copybook Headings" by Rudyard Kipling.

60. See http://teachingamericanhistory.org/library/index.asp?document=41

61. *Ibid.*

62. The oft-quoted epithet is from W. H. Auden's poem, "September 1, 1939." See http://www.goodreads.com/quotes/show/2492

63. This sounds wrong in light of common assumptions about the impact of 1960s civil-rights legislation and anti-poverty programs. But the data support the assertion, as shown by Charles Murray in *Losing Ground: American Social Policy 1950-1980* (New York: Basic Books, 1984). For an overview of the book in Murray's own words two years later, see http://www.cato.org/pubs/journal/cj6n1/cj6n1-2.pdf

64. See *Camelot and the Cultural Revolution* by James Piereson (New York: Encounter Books, 2007)

65. That very indictment of America, in that very year, was what I sought to refute in my *GE Forum* point-counterpoint with Carl Oglesby; see Chapter 6.

66. Alexis de Tocqueville, *Democracy in America*, Reeve translation edited by Philips Bradley (New York: Knopf, 1945), vol. 2, pp. 318-319

67. *Ibid.*

68. See http://www.whitehouse.gov/the-press-office/
    president-barack-obamas-inaugural-address

69. Sir John Glubb, *The Fate of Empires and Search for Survival* (Edinburgh: William
    Blackwood, 1978), p. 28.

70. The full quotation reads: "This was the object of the Declaration of Independence. Not
    to find out new principles, or new arguments, never before thought of, not merely to
    say things which had never been said before; but to place before mankind the common
    sense of the subject, in terms so plain and firm as to command their assent, and to
    justify ourselves in the independent stand we are compelled to take. Neither aiming at
    originality of principle or sentiment, nor yet copied from any particular and previous
    writing, it was intended to be an expression of the American mind, and to give to
    that expression the proper tone and spirit called for by the occasion." See http://www.
    savingtheusconstitution.com/thomas_jefferson_quotes.html

71. With Ben Wattenberg's 1990 book entitled *The First Universal Nation* (New York: Free
    Press), this useful if debatable phrase entered our language.

72. See http://www.jewishvirtuallibrary.org/jsource/Quote/hillel2.html

73. See http://quotes.liberty-tree.ca/quotes_by/frederic+bastiat

74. See Matthew 22:21, Exodus 20:3, and Psalms 146:3 (all King James Version)

75. In a 2003 article entitled "A Case for Divided Government," Cato Institute economist
    William Niskanen laid out the evidence that one-party rule in Washington, whether by
    Democrats or Republicans, tends to accelerate the growth of government. See http://
    www.cato.org/pub_display.php?pub_id=3088

76. From Kipling's 1919 poem, "The Gods of the Copybook Headings;" see full text in
    Appendix.

77. See http://www.goodreads.com/work/quotes/

78. From a letter of Jefferson to Benjamin Rush, Sept. 23, 1800. See Andrew A. Lipscomb,
    Ed., *The Writings of Thomas Jefferson* (Washington: Thomas Jefferson Memorial
    Association, 1907), Vol. 10, p. 175

79. The quotation is from Lincoln's Lyceum Address of 1838; see http://
    teachingamericanhistory.org/library/index.asp?document=157

80. See http://www.whitehouse.gov/the-press-office/
    president-barack-obamas-inaugural-address

81. See Eugene Burdick and William Lederer, *The Ugly American* (New York: Norton, 1958)

ACKNOWLEDGMENTS

THEY HELPED ME BUILD

James Andrews, my brother, and Brian Kennedy of the Claremont Institute, encouraged me to step back from the daily routine and make this book a reality. Don Siecke provided the ideal quiet office for my writer's retreat.

Dean Singleton of the *Denver Post* and Brian Taylor of KNUS Radio gave me the platform as a pundit to develop the vision of "Element R." Kevin Miller of the National Freedom Initiative helped me hone that vision, and introduced me to Denali Press.

Rebecca Fox was a discerning editor and a fast friend. Denali's Rex Rolf ably saw the book into print. Joyce Beckett and Karthik Venkatraj, our Centennial Institute staff, smoothed my path down the homestretch.

Above all, Donna, the love of my life, and Tina, Jen, and Daniel, our children, deserve a heavenly crown for keeping faith with me when others might not have, as I learned the meaning of personal responsibility the hard way.

*By wisdom is an house builded.... and in
multitude of counsellors there is safety.*
—Proverbs 24:6

*Of making many books there is no end.... Let us hear the conclusion
of the whole matter: Fear God, and keep his commandments:
For this is the whole duty [responsibility] of man.*
—Ecclesiastes 12:12,13

JOHN ANDREWS has been a leading conservative voice in his generation since the 1960s. Today he is director of the Centennial Institute, a think tank at Colorado Christian University.

In past years he served as President of the Colorado Senate, helped enact his state's widely-imitated Taxpayer Bill of Rights, and founded the Independence Institute, a leading national voice for liberty.

Andrews does daily commentary for Colorado Public Television, writes for the *Denver Post*, and originated Backbone Radio. As a former chairman of State Policy Network, he consults widely for legislative leaders.

Earlier John was a speechwriter for President Nixon, an appointee of President Ronald Reagan and President George W. Bush—and he ran for Governor of Colorado as the Republican nominee in 1990.

He also launched TCI Cable News, served as editor of *Imprimis* at Hillsdale College, and was a senior executive with two Christian ministries.

He grew up in the Colorado mountains, graduated from Principia College, and served as a US Navy submarine officer. He and Donna, his wife of 44 years, have three grown children and a grandson.